TWAYNE'S WORLD AUTHORS SERIES

A Survey of the World's Literature

Sylvia E. Bowman, Indiana University

GENERAL EDITOR

SPAIN

Gerald E. Wade, Vanderbilt University
Janet Winecoff Díaz, University of North Carolina

EDITORS

Diego de San Pedro

(TWAS 310)

Diego de San Pedro

By KEITH WHINNOM

University of Exeter, England

Twayne Publishers, Inc.   ::   New York

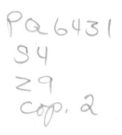

Library of Congress Cataloging in Publication Data

Whinnom, Keith, 1927–
  Diego de San Pedro.

  (Twayne's world authors series, TWAS 310. Spain)
  Bibliography: p. 155.
  1. San Pedro, Diego de, fl. 1500.
PQ6431.S4Z9   868'.2'09 [B]   73-22096
ISBN 0-8057-2788-4

To Edward M. Wilson

Preface

Diego de San Pedro is without doubt one of the most important and influential figures in the history of Spanish, and indeed European literature: his imagination directly affected the imagination of writers in Spanish, French, Italian, English, and German for over a century after his death. As an innovator he does not quite rank with a Petrarch or a Boccaccio, but he does not lag far behind. And yet, though generations of scholars have acknowledged the originality of his contribution to literature, singularly little of any substance has been written about him; the larger part of what has been written has tended to concentrate on aspects of his prose works; and too many historians of literature have chosen to comment petulantly on the "artificiality" of his writings while neglecting to explain the phenomenal popularity which his works enjoyed both in the Peninsula and in Europe generally. The present volume is, indeed, the first to make an attempt to describe and evaluate the man and his literary output as a whole.

About San Pedro and his works I have written extensively elsewhere, most especially in the introductions to the three-volume edition of his *Obras completas* now in course of publication by Editorial Castalia (Madrid); but even on the pretext of introducing him to a non-Spanish speaking public, a simple translation of those prologues could hardly have been justified. There I was concerned with introducing individual texts, with sundry technicalities such as bibliographical and textual problems, and with trying to remove a series of traditional misconceptions and misinterpretations. Here, although there is inevitably some overlap, most particularly in Chapter 1, and although I have indicated the existence of areas of controversy, I have assumed no prior knowledge (or misinformation) on the part of the reader, and I have endeavored simply to present a coherent picture of the man, of his writings, and of the extraordinary period of Spanish history through which he lived.

I have supplied references for those who may wish to pursue further some of the problems with which students of this remarkable writer are still faced; but the English-speaking reader should be warned that the larger part of the critical literature is in Spanish and that, as yet, no modern English translations exist of the works themselves. Given the limitations of space in the present series, I have chosen to sacrifice the discussion of problems which can be properly approached and pursued only by those with an adequate knowledge of modern and fifteenth-century Spanish.

A study of San Pedro's writings reveals a literary personality behind which one glimpses a human being of rare talent and unusual sensitivity. The impact which Diego de San Pedro made on sixteenth-century Europe can be attributed to various different factors. Not the least important is the new prestige which Spain and the Spanish language acquired in the reigns of Ferdinand and Isabella, and Charles V. But San Pedro distinguished himself among his compatriots, not even excepting Fernando de Rojas, author of *Celestina*, and his literary personality is marked by two insistent characteristics which undoubtedly contributed to his success. One is a hypersensitivity to criticism coupled with a genuine desire to please: San Pedro was a professional long before any man could call writing his profession; he responded immediately, in an age of drastic and radical change, to each fresh breeze of fashion. His response, indeed—and this is the second characteristic of his literary personality—came close to being overresponsiveness; time and again he discarded the old in order to push the new to its logical conclusion. Repeatedly, therefore, the critic is driven to employ superlatives ... which are by no means always complimentary. So, for instance, San Pedro's one excursion into obscenity produces not only the most obscene poem in the *Cancionero general* but even the most outrageous in that scabrous collection known as the *Obras de burlas*. Extremism is a constant in virtually all his work; and if he does not reach some extreme at the first attempt he will reach it at the second.

In this volume I attempt, consecutively, to identify the man historically, to sketch the features of the age of ferment in which he lived, and then to describe and evaluate, in chrono-

Preface

logical order, the works in which San Pedro reacted, in his highly individual manner, to the ideas, aspirations, styles, fashions, and moods of his own time.

As I well know from the comments of many generations of students, there are certain barriers which intervene between Diego de San Pedro and his modern readers. But I believe that they can be overcome. Furthermore, if I may be permitted a purely personal observation, I find that Diego de San Pedro wears well. Long after one has exhausted, through repeated readings and explanations, one's enthusiasm even for such a remarkable and popular work as *Celestina,* one finds that Diego de San Pedro retains his freshness. To endeavor to explain just why this is so is one of the main purposes of this volume.

KEITH WHINNOM

University of Exeter

Contents

Chronology

1456 Birth of the twins Don Juan and Don Rodrigo Téllez-Girón; legitimization by Papal Bull of Calixtus III.

1464 Don Pedro Girón, planning to marry the Princess Isabella, cedes the Grand Mastership of Calatrava to his son Rodrigo.

1465 Deposition of King Henry IV of Castile; Civil War.

1466 Death of Don Pedro Girón; his eldest son, Don Alfonso, becomes Count of Urueña.

1469 Death of Don Alfonso Téllez-Girón; Don Juan Téllez-Girón becomes Count of Urueña. Marriage of Ferdinand and Isabella.

1472 The Téllez-Girón twins come of age; Don Rodrigo assumes personal control of the Military Order of Calatrava.

1474 Death of King Henry IV; disputed accession of Isabella; invasion of Castile by the Portuguese; the Téllez-Girón twins support "La Beltraneja"; siege of Peñafiel. First book printed in Spain (in Valencia). Approximate date for the composition of San Pedro's *Pasión trovada* (*Versified Passion*).

1476 Reorganization of the Santa Hermandad. The Téllez-Girón twins submit to Isabella.

1478 Establishment of the Spanish Inquisition.

1479 Death of John II of Aragon; accession of Ferdinand; union of Castile and Aragon.

1481 Probable date of composition of San Pedro's *Arnalte y Lucenda* (*Arnalte and Lucenda*).

1482 Beginning of the war against Granada. Don Rodrigo Téllez-Girón is killed at the siege of Loja.

1483 Battle of Lucena; the Alcaide de los Donceles takes King Boabdil prisoner.

1485 Approximate date for the composition of San Pedro's *Sermón* (*Sermon*).

1486 Reconquest of Málaga.

1488 Embassy from Burgundy; Baldwin of Burgundy contracts marriage with Doña Marina Manuel. Approximate date for the composition of San Pedro's *Cárcel de Amor* (*Prison of Love*).

1491 First known edition of *Arnalte and Lucenda*.

1492   Capitulation of Granada. Expulsion of all Jews from Spain. Discovery of America by Columbus. First known edition of *Prison of Love*; first recorded printing (now lost) of *The Versified Passion*; and first recorded separate printing of *Las siete angustias de Nuestra Señora* (*The Seven Sorrows of Our Lady*).

1493   Catalan translation of *Prison of Love* (*Lo Carcer de Amor*).

1495   Baldwin of Burgundy returns to Spain. Naples is occupied by the French. First known editions of Juan de Flores's *Grimalte y Gradissa* and *Grisel y Mirabella*.

1496   Baldwin of Burgundy acts as proxy for Philip the Handsome in marrying Princess Juana. Publication of *Prison of Love* with a continuation by Nicolás Núñez.

1497   Death of the heir apparent, Prince John. Expulsion of all Jews from Portugal.

1498   Possible date of composition of San Pedro's *Desprecio de la Fortuna* (*Contempt of Fortune*).

1499   First known edition of *La comedia de Calisto y Melibea* (the short version of *Celestina*).

1500   Rising of the Moors of the Alpujarras.

1501   Expedition of Don Juan Téllez-Girón against the Moors of the Sierra Bermeja. Partition of Naples by France and Spain.

1502   War between Spain and France. Expulsion of all Muslims from Spain. Date of *La tragicomedia de Calisto y Melibea* (the expanded version of *Celestina*).

1504   Death of Isabella; accession of Philip and Juana. Defeat of the French in Italy.

1505   Ferdinand assumes the Regency; plot against him organized by Don Juan Manuel II.

1506   Death of Philip the Handsome. Death of Columbus. First known printing of San Pedro's *Contempt of Fortune*.

1507   Queen Juana, insane, is incarcerated at Tordesillas.

1508   Opening of the University of Alcalá.

1509   Conquest of Oran.

1511   *Cancionero general* of Hernando del Castillo: first known printing of San Pedro's minor poems; first recorded printing (now lost) of his *Sermon*.

1512   Conquest and incorporation of the Kingdom of Navarre.

1513   Balboa discovers the Pacific.

1515   Italian translation of *Prison of Love* (*Carcer d'amore*).

1516   Death of Ferdinand; accession of Charles I.

1517   Charles I arrives in Spain.

Chronology

1518   Fray Alberto de Aguayo dedicates his translation of Boethius to Don Juan Téllez-Girón.

1519   Charles I becomes the Emperor Charles V.

1520   Excommunication of Luther.

1525   French translation of *Prison of Love* (*Prison d'amour*).

1526   The Venetian ambassador, Navagiero, visits Don Juan Téllez-Girón in Osuna.

1528   Death of Don Juan Téllez-Girón.

CHAPTER 1

The Man

1 Which Diego de San Pedro?

THERE can be few major European writers of whom we
know less than of Diego de San Pedro. The details of his
life, and the dates of his birth and death, are no more than a
matter of conjecture. It is true that in most of the standard
encyclopedias and histories of literature he is equipped with a
biography of sorts, but this is because around 1905 Marcelino
Menéndez Pelayo confused our author with another man of the
same name, belonging to a generation earlier than the writer's;[1]
and, indeed, Menéndez Pelayo was himself correcting yet another misidentification, made by the great seventeenth-century
bibliographer, Nicolás Antonio, who thought that the author of
Cárcel de Amor (*Prison of Love*) was a poet of the reign of
John II (1406–1454).[2]

Despite the notorious unreliability of the source of Nicolás
Antonio's information, José Pellicer's *Informe del origen, anti-
güedad, calidad i sucesión de la excelentíssima Casa de Sarmiento de Villamayor y las unidas a ella por casamiento* (*A Report
of the Origins, Antiquity, Nobility, and Genealogy of the Most
Distinguished Family of Sarmiento de Villamayor and of the
Families Linked with It by Marriage*), printed in Madrid in
1663, there can be little doubt that a poet by the name of Diego
de San Pedro, an alderman (*regidor,* or *decurio* in Nicolás Antonio's Latin) of the city of Valladolid, did compose a long
poem, now lost, entitled *El libro de los llantos* (*The Book of
Laments*), in the meter known as *arte mayor,* and dedicated it
to King John II.[3] But it is equally clear that this man cannot
be the author of any of the extant works which are attributed to
"Diego de San Pedro," since they were obviously written at a
much later date.

17

The man whom we may call the "second" Diego de San Pedro (though there are at least half a dozen Diego de San Pedros to be found in the fifteenth century) was a figure of some importance and his name appears in a series of documents. We know that he held the degree of *bachiller* (in the fifteenth century a university Bachelor, rather than the modern high-school graduate), that he was castellan or governor (*alcaide*) of the fortress of Peñafiel (east of Valladolid), which belonged to the formidable Don Pedro Girón, that he was a judge (*oidor del rey*), and that he was a "lieutenant" (*teniente*: officer with deputed authority) of Don Pedro. He is first referred to, as castellan of Peñafiel, in a document dated 1459, and he is repeatedly mentioned in sundry other documents (including the will of Don Pedro Girón, drawn up in 1466) until 1472. Thereafter he disappears completely from our knowledge, and it is almost certain that he must have died in 1472 or shortly thereafter, since his epitaph in Peñafiel, copied by investigators in 1592, refers only to his service with Don Pedro Girón.[4]

There are just two slim and unsatisfactory reasons for supposing that this man was our author. One is that at the end of *Prison of Love*, the author, concluding his tale, writes: "I arrived here in Peñafiel"; and in the prose prologue to his poem on Fortune, *Desprecio de la Fortuna* (*Contempt of Fortune*), he mentions that he has spent twenty-nine years in the service of Don Juan Téllez-Girón (one of the sons of Don Pedro).[5] The one coincidence of some significance is, of course, the allusion to Peñafiel, but when we discover that in 1467 there were actually two men named Diego de San Pedro living in Peñafiel (one the *bachiller* and *teniente*), we begin to see the implausibility of attributing the writings of "Diego de San Pedro" to the lieutenant of Don Pedro Girón. (The document in question, copied by the investigators of 1592, is a list of the members of the *Cofradía de los Hidalgos de Peñafiel*, Association of the Gentry of Peñafiel, and it is perhaps worth noting that besides the *bachiller-teniente*, mentioned first, and clearly the most important person in the town, there figure in this list a Diego de San Pedro, a Juan and an Alonso de San Pedro, and a *comendador*, or knight-commander, San Pedro.)[6]

In every other respect, what we know of Don Pedro Girón's

lieutenant fails to accord with what we must deduce about our author. In a period when a writer who held a degree scarcely ever failed to advertise the fact on the title page of his books, our poet and novelist does not mention his being a *bachiller*;[7] furthermore, he never once refers to Don Pedro Girón, and on one occasion maintains a conspicuous silence when it would have been natural to give his name, for in the defense of women placed in the mouth of Leriano in *Prison of Love,* San Pedro cites as a shining example of virtue the mistress of Don Pedro, Isabel de las Casas, but in these terms: "Doña Isabella, mother of the Grand Master of the Order of Calatrava, Don Rodrigo Téllez-Girón, and of the two Counts of Urueña, Don Alonso and Don Juan."[8] When we recall also that the bachelor-lieutenant's tombstone speaks of his being in the service only of Don Pedro, and that the author writes of his being twenty-nine years in the service of his son, Don Juan, we perceive that there must have been a gap of at least one generation between the two. The *bachiller* vanishes from history six years after the death of his master Don Pedro, and our author, a servant of his son, could not have begun writing before the 1470's, about the time the other Diego de San Pedro must have died, and he continued writing, for the ladies and gentlemen of the court of Queen Isabella, into the 1480's and 1490's.[9]

It is undoubtedly tempting to see in the "other" Diego de San Pedro of the 1467 list the first documentary allusion to our author, but there is no really firm evidence on which we can rely. It is also tempting to suppose that the *bachiller* and the poet must have been related in some way (possibly uncle and nephew, since the documents of 1592 say the *bachiller* had no children), but this is again the merest speculation. When it comes to putting down concrete facts about the life of the writer, there is very little more that we can say.

II *Was Diego de San Pedro Jewish?*

It is habitually affirmed in the standard works of reference that Diego de San Pedro was a *converso,* that is to say, a Jew converted to Christianity, or the descendant of such a converted Jew. Given his somewhat suspect surname and his presumed profession (he must have been some sort of secretary or administrative assistant to the Count of Urueña), there is nothing inherently implausible in the proposition, but there is hardly a shred of concrete evidence to support it. Menéndez Pelayo took note in his omnivorous reading of two rather unlikely anecdotes related by the notoriously malicious, irresponsible, and quite unreliable Luis Zapata, who composed his Miscelánea (Miscellany) while serving a twenty-year jail sentence and had it printed in 1592.[10] In neither of these little tales does Zapata name Diego de San Pedro. He refers only to "the man who wrote the Passion in verse," el que trobó la Pasión. And while it is true that San Pedro's Pasión trovada (Versified Passion) was easily the most popular of a dozen or more versified Passions composed before the date of Zapata's Miscellany, it is also quite clear that he is not the only possible candidate.[11] Eugenio Asensio believes, in fact, that Zapata intended to allude to Jorge de Montemayor,[12] who was widely reputed to be of Jewish stock. Furthermore, Asensio has pointed out that the first of these two rather feeble jokes is to be found earlier, with no mention of the subject's being the composer of a versified Passion, in Juan Timoneda.

Subsequently, Emilio Cotarelo y Mori found a group of documents in the Archivo Histórico Nacional of Madrid, investigations into the lineage of various members of the well-known Fonseca family, which in his view proved that Diego de San Pedro was a converso.[13] He ignored not only the conclusions of the investigators themselves, but every scrap of evidence which militated against his thesis.[14] Furthermore, the original investigators, and, of course, Cotarelo himself, had the bachiller and teniente inextricably confused with the author of Prison of Love and The Versified Passion, although the informants in Peñafiel either did not know that the previous governor of their town and fortress had been a writer, or did not know that the man who wrote Prison of Love was one of the more famous earlier inhabitants of Peñafiel.

The whole investigation is full of red herrings, and Cotarelo failed to notice the testimony which shows them for what they are. So, for instance, he ignores the fact that an assertion that one Pedro Suárez de Toledo, known as Pedro Suárez de San Pedro, was the brother of Diego the poet is demonstrably false, since, as the witnesses examined in Jerez de la Frontera explained, Pedro Suárez's parents gave him the name of "Saint Peter" as a pious gesture after all their other children had died. Similarly, Cotarelo omits to mention that a commoner called Juan de San Pedro, resident in Peñafiel in the early sixteenth century, was not only *falsely* accused of judaizing practices (his accuser fled for sanctuary to Galicia, to Santiago de Compostela, and denied that he had ever made such a charge), but could have had nothing to do with the author, since he arrived in Peñafiel, certainly after the author's death, as plain Juan Llezo, and came to be known as Juan de San Pedro because he came from the village of San Pedro de Yanguas; that he had a son called Diego de San Pedro is irrelevant. A shopkeeping Diego de San Pedro of Peñafiel, whose wife Constance was condemned as an apostate judaizing heretic in 1494, is also quite obviously not our author.

All that does emerge from these hundreds of pages of testimony, and from a fourth investigation discovered later by the Marquis del Saltillo,[15] is that three irresponsible witnesses, who can be proved to have made other wildly inaccurate statements, said that a man called San Pedro (either Diego or Pedro), identified as the author of *The Versified Passion* or of *Prison of Love*, was of Jewish descent. None of these witnesses was resident in Peñafiel, and scores of other witnesses, including parish priests and officers of the Military Orders, were ready to affirm that "Diego de San Pedro" was not a *converso*. The testimony of these other witnesses cannot, unfortunately, be held to be conclusive either. They were not only almost a century removed in time from our author, but were also thoroughly confused about the *bachiller*'s being the writer. The confusion was inevitable since it was written into the list of questions asked of every witness in Peñafiel ("Was the *bachiller* and *alcaide* Diego de San Pedro, author of *Prison of Love*, of Jewish descent?"), but it means that the answers elicited cannot be relied on. Moreover, it is possible and even probable that our Diego de San Pedro left Peñafiel for Osuna in 1492, to be with his master Don Juan.

It has been argued that San Pedro's surname is suspect, and

it is undoubtedly true that many Jews converted to Christianity
in the course of the fourteenth and fifteenth centuries did take
new baptismal names like "San Pedro" or "Santa María," illustri-
ous Castilian names like Mendoza, place-names like "de Montal-
bán," or simply the name of their *padrino* (godfather, or
baptismal sponsor). On the other hand, not only was there a
family of the lesser Castilian nobility called San Pedro, originally
from Cantabria[16] (and therefore unlikely to be of Jewish origin,
even though nobility and Jewishness were indeed not incom-
patible), but the investigations discovered by Cotarelo provide
us with at least two clear examples of how the name of "San
Pedro" was adopted by or applied to individuals who were, on
the available evidence, not "new Christians" at all: the villager
Juan Llezo from San Pedro de Yanguas, and the knight-commander Pedro Suárez de Toledo.[17]

In any event, it is not easy to see what difference San Pedro's
origins make to the interpretation of his writings. Márquez
Villanueva has argued that *Prison of Love* is, in part at least,
a "political novel," in that the episode involving the arbitrary,
cruel, and manifestly unjust verdict of the King, combated by
the Cardinal and others, is a veiled attack on the operations of
the Inquisition.[18] Certainly some of the arguments mustered
on Laureola's behalf could be employed, if not construed, as
an indictment of some of the procedures of the Spanish
Inquisition. But this interpretation of the novel does not
entirely convince.

We must conclude that while there is no strong evidence
that Diego de San Pedro did *not* have some Jewish blood in
his veins, there is, equally, no shred of incontrovertible evidence
that he had.

III *Don Juan Téllez-Girón*

As I have indicated, we have almost no positive information
about the details of our author's life; but one firm statement,
made by the author himself, we *can* rely on, and that is that,
at the time of writing the prologue to his *Contempt of Fortune,*
he had spent twenty-nine years in the service of Don Juan Téllez-
Girón, Count of Urueña. Some details of the Count's life will not

be without relevance in filling in the background of our author's biography.

Don Juan was one of the originally illegitimate sons of Don Pedro Girón, Grand Master of the Military Order of Calatrava, who was with his brother Don Juan Pacheco, Marquis of Villena, Grand Master of the Order of Santiago, and favorite of King Henry IV (1454–1474), one of the richest and most powerful grandees of his time.[19] By the most shameless exploitation and manipulation of the situation created by the problem of the succession—for the daughter of Queen Juana of Portugal, Henry's wife, was alleged by many grandees to be not the daughter of the King, but of his favorite Beltrán de la Cueva (whence she was known as Juana "la Beltraneja")—Don Pedro placed the King in such straits that he consented to the marriage of Don Pedro with his own younger sister Isabella (later Queen Isabella the Catholic), whom he recognized as heir to the throne. Don Pedro failed to become Prince Consort and joint ruler of Castile only because he died of a heart attack on his way to the wedding. Even Dr. Gudiel, the usually flattering chronicler of the fortunes of the Girón family, takes note of the widely diffused story that Don Pedro died in answer to the prayers of the young Princess.[20] The humiliation to which Isabella was subjected at this time may be one reason why Diego de San Pedro scrupulously avoids mentioning the name of Don Pedro in *Prison of Love*, as I noted above.

By his mistress, Isabel de las Casas,[21] Don Pedro left three sons: Alfonso, born in 1453, and the twins Juan and Rodrigo Téllez-Girón, born in 1456. All were legitimized by a Papal Bull of Calixtus III and subsequently by a royal decree of Henry IV. Since marriage was prohibited to the Grand Master of the Order of Calatrava, Don Pedro, clearly already thinking of a union with the Princess Isabella, ceded his Grand-Mastership to his son Rodrigo (then eight years old) in 1464, and had King Henry create for Alfonso the earldom of Urueña.[22] But Alfonso died in his sixteenth year, in 1469, and Juan Téllez-Girón inherited, at the age of twelve, the title of Count of Urueña, along with sundry other titles held by his deceased father: Lord of Osuna, Piedra, Peñafiel, and so on.[23] It is to be presumed that, as in the case of his twin Rodrigo, who did not personally assume command of the Order of Calatrava until he was sixteen, Juan's guardians, Enrique de Figueredo (Don Pedro's chancellor) and Don Juan Pacheco, managed his affairs until he too attained his majority in 1472. This would explain why the tomb of the *bachiller* San Pedro failed to mention any master but Don Pedro.

On the death of Henry IV in 1474, the young Giróns, under the influence of their cousin Don Diego López Pacheco, Marquis of Villena (son of Don Juan Pacheco, who also died in 1474, just before the King), their uncle Alfonso Carrillo, Archbishop of Toledo, and other nobles, decided to support the faction of Juana "la Beltraneja," in opposition to Isabella. But the allegiances of the Girón clan were split; there were family connections in Isabella's party also; and the twins abandoned the cause of Juana in 1476 and signed an agreement on May 22 with Isabella, who promised them complete indemnity.[24] The Constable of Castile, Pedro Fernández de Velasco, Count of Haro, whose son Bernardino had already married the Téllez-Giróns's cousin, Catalina Pacheco,[25] was instrumental in effecting the reconciliation and gave his own daughter in marriage to Juan Téllez-Girón. This lady, Leonor de la Vega y Velasco, was on her mother's side a granddaughter of the Marquis of Santillana, and her extreme devoutness may be held partly responsible, as we shall see, for Diego de San Pedro's later condemnation of all his own frivolous writings.

The Girón twins did not assist Isabella against the rival claimant to her throne, but did subsequently throw themselves wholeheartedly into the war against Granada, which Isabella started in 1482. Rodrigo in a very short space of time—for he was killed at the siege of Loja that same year—acquired a tremendous reputation for fearless courage, and there are at least fifteen ballads extant recording his exploits.[26] After the death of his beloved twin brother, Don Juan put ever greater efforts into the pursuit of the war, expending men and money recklessly in the desire, it is alleged, to avenge his brother's death. When Granada finally capitulated on January 2, 1492, Don Juan entered the city alongside Ferdinand and Isabella, and it was he, as *Notario Mayor* (roughly Attorney General,

an office held earlier by his father), who authorized the
capitulatory documents.

There is good circumstantial evidence that Diego de San
Pedro also played some part in the campaign against Granada.
No chronicler records his presence, but one of the Peñafiel
witnesses of 1592 speaks confusedly (the recording scribe has
made some error) of a Diego de San Pedro's service in Granada,
and at the beginning of *Prison of Love* he writes that the adventure began as he was returning home through the Sierra Morena
(to Peñafiel, as it subsequently appears), "after last year's campaign." The mention of the Sierra Morena means that the war
alluded to can only be the Granada campaign, and although
this evidence is far from conclusive, San Pedro's descriptions of
military maneuvers in *Prison of Love* (the armed rescue of Laureola from jail, the tactical retreat, the siege of Susa, and so on)
do suggest that he had some personal familiarity with fifteenth-
century warfare, and it would be in no way surprising if he had
in fact accompanied his master through at least some of the
summer campaigns. We shall return to our author's later years
in the service of Don Juan, but in order to deal with matters
in chronological order we should look first at two other members of the nobility with whom San Pedro was acquainted.

IV *The Alcaide de los Donceles and Doña Marina Manuel*

Diego de San Pedro dedicated *Prison of Love* to Diego Fernández de Córdoba, seventh Alcaide de los Donceles. The
donceles or "young gentlemen," were, in this context, a troop
of light cavalry composed solely of young noblemen who enjoyed
certain special privileges. The Alcaide, their leader, was not
necessarily a young man, for Don Diego's father, Martín Fernández de Córdoba, held the same post, as sixth Alcaide, up to
his death in 1469. Don Diego, however, could not have been
older than twenty when Isabella opened hostilities against
Granada, for in 1462 his father made a will to the effect that
if God should be pleased to give him sons, the eldest should
be his heir.[27] The young man achieved fame early, when in
1483 he won the battle of Lucena and took prisoner King Boabdil
of Granada, and he was to go on later to achieve even greater

fame and power. Inevitably the Alcaide's presence coincided with that of Don Juan Téllez-Girón, and probably of Diego de San Pedro, in numerous battles and sieges.[28]

But there were also family links between the Girón and Fernández de Córdoba families. In 1476 the widowed Catalina Pacheco, Don Juan's cousin, married the Alcaide's uncle, Alfonso Fernández de Córdoba de Aguilar, "the Great" (see note 25); more important, the Alcaide himself married Catalina's younger half-sister Juana. We do not know when this marriage took place, but the contract could have been made at any time after 1475, when Juana's engagement to the heir apparent to the Portuguese throne was broken off. All this is not without relevance when it comes to the problem of establishing the dating and chronology of San Pedro's writings.

Apart from Queen Isabella, Diego Fernández de Córdoba, and members of the Girón family, the only other person mentioned by name in the works of San Pedro is Doña Marina Manuel.[29] He refers to her in these terms in the prologue to *Prison of Love*: "I was told that I should write something in the style of a discourse [he means his *Sermon*] which I sent to the Lady Marina Manuel, since she found it superior to the style I employed in another novel of mine which she read."[30] Doña Marina belonged to the very highest Castilian nobility, being ultimately a descendant of King Ferdinand III, "St. Ferdinand," of Castile (1217–1252). She was the great-granddaughter of Don Juan Manuel (1282–1348), writer, and Regent of Castile during the minority of Alfonso XI; and her mother, Aldonza de la Vega, was a great-aunt of Garcilaso de la Vega, the poet. Moreover, she was related by marriage to Don Juan Téllez-Girón, who had married Doña Leonor de la Vega y Velasco, of the same distinguished family of the Lasso de la Vega. At some date which I have not yet determined, but between 1489 and 1495, Doña Marina was married, as part of the cementation of the Burgundian alliance, to Baldwin of Burgundy, one of the bastard half-brothers of Charles the Bold. Before departing for Flanders she served as one of Queen Isabella's attendant ladies, at least until 1490,[31] and in the fever of literary composition which infected possibly the greater part of the nobility at the court of Isabella,[32] made her own very modest contribution in the form of a *mote* which was glossed by the poet Cartagena.[33] In short, it would seem on the available evidence that Diego de San Pedro's acquaintance with the great nobility of his time was limited to the family of the Téllez-Giróns and to certain individuals connected with it by marriage.

V *The Years of Decline*

Granada capitulated on January 2, 1492. Don Juan Téllez-Girón, who had suffered in the course of the campaign immense losses of both men and money, retired to his estates in Andalusia to attempt to establish some order in his affairs. His wife, Doña Leonor de la Vega, had always been, it would seem, deeply religious, and on returning from the wars Don Juan also began to demonstrate the most noteworthy piety, most particularly in further dispersing his wealth to alleviate the lot of the poor. The references we have to Don Juan's charity and devoutness do seem to go beyond the clichés of ordinary panegyric and to reflect something more striking and even extravagant.[34]

It must have been in this period that Diego de San Pedro began to repent of his "frivolous writings" (*obras livianas*) and to follow his master in sober reflections upon the meaning and purpose of life. In the prose prologue to his *Contempt of Fortune* he writes: "It was easier to find a worthy recipient of these verses than to write them, for I can truly say, with no intent to flatter, that there is no man alive who displays more rectitude, or who has so wisely exchanged the goods of this world for the hope of rewards in the next."[35]

Don Juan Téllez-Girón was not permitted to live entirely free from the responsibilities of his birth. In 1501 he was summoned to lead a brief campaign against the rebel Moors of the Sierra Bermeja, from which he barely escaped with his life, while Don Alonso de Aguilar (uncle of the Alcaide de los Donceles) perished.[36] In 1505, after the death of Isabella, Doña Marina Manuel's brother, Don Juan Manuel II, accounted one of the wiliest diplomats in Europe, involved him in the plot against Ferdinand, who had assumed the Regency.[37] Thereafter, however, Don Juan lived quite retired from the court and affairs of state. In 1526, not long before he died in 1528, he was visited in his home at Osuna by the Venetian Ambassador Navagiero (whose chance remarks to Boscán were to have important consequences for Spanish literature). Navagiero found him "very old" (*molto vecchio*—he was, in fact, seventy) "but still a perfect courtier" (*e gentil cortegiano però*).[38] His wife, Leonor, had died in 1522; the Alcaide de los Donceles VII died in 1518; Don Juan almost certainly outlived San Pedro also.

When Diego de San Pedro died we do not know, except that it must have been after 1498, the earliest date at which he could have written his *Contempt of Fortune*.[39] If we are to believe what he says in that work, he died in reduced circumstances; certainly he died in obscurity, his death unnoticed and unrecorded by a younger generation.

CHAPTER 2

An Age of Transition

I *Spain in Turmoil*

THE sorry tale of Spanish history in the earlier part of the fifteenth century, in the reigns of John II and his son Henry IV, is one we need not pursue in detail.[1] Socially, politically, and economically, Castile appeared to be lapsing rapidly into decadence, and it seemed that her feeble rulers could do nothing to arrest the decline into anarchy which had begun in the fourteenth century and which reached its shameful climax in the latter part of the reign of Henry IV. From the beginning of the century, droughts, famines, further sporadic outbreaks of the plague, debasement of the coinage, and consequent gross rises in the cost of staple foods led to a series of popular uprisings, lynchings, and massacres, frequently directed (as they were elsewhere in Europe) against the Jews and the *conversos*.[2] Throughout the land, brigandage, robbery, and violence were rife, and justice was held in contempt. Great nobles could wage private wars with private armies, unheeding of royal authority. The Cortes were divided, weak, and ineffectual. The Church was immensely wealthy; its prelates were too frequently worldly politicians; and its clergy was uneducated, indolent, and often flagrantly dissolute. The court and the monarchy itself, most particularly in the person of Henry IV, were self-indulgent, extravagant, and licentious. The notorious homosexual proclivities of the King, his alleged impotence, and the Queen's barely concealed affairs with sundry lovers, were matters of popular "knowledge" and doubtless lost little in the telling.[3] Henry IV was ignominiously deposed in 1465 in favor of his brother Alfonso, the noble conspirators alleging gross misrule and claiming that they could not consent to the succession of the Queen's daughter Juana because she could not possibly be the daughter of the King. Don Pedro Girón, for personal advantage, switched his allegiance back to the King, and civil war raged intermittently up to and beyond the death of Pedro Girón in 1466, of Prince Alfonso in 1468, of Henry in 1474, and the accession of Isabella.

The Crown of Aragon, finally united with Castile under Ferdinand and Isabella, was hardly in better case. At the beginning of the century a problem of succession was resolved without civil war; under the second ruler of the new dynasty, Alfonso the Magnanimous (1416–1458), there occurred a new period of expansion in which a large part of Italy, including Sardinia, Sicily, and the Kingdom of Naples, was acquired by the Catalan-Aragonese Federation; and at home complex procedures and a skilled corps of administrators ensured that government ran smoothly, that the Cortes played their full part, and that no problems arose in maintaining public order or exercising effective political control. But if in the first half of the century the history of Aragon was happier than that of Castile, there were grave underlying problems, and decline came swiftly from the middle of the century on. The alien dynasty was never popular with the Catalans, and the estrangement of the King from the people was grossly exacerbated in 1443 by King Alfonso's decision to move his court to Naples. Furthermore, Catalonia, the economic mainspring of the Federation, was repeatedly and remorselessly struck by recurrences of the plague, from which that area suffered far more than Castile, Aragon, or Valencia, so that farms were abandoned and agrarian unrest manifested itself in the murder of landlords and the burning of crops and farmsteads. Even the impressive commercial and urban wealth of the County of Barcelona, resting largely on its textile industry, began to be adversely affected toward the middle of the century by the growth of piracy, by competition from the Genoese, by financial crisis, and by the exorbitant demands of Alfonso the Magnanimous for more money to satisfy his imperial ambitions. Under John II of Aragon (1458–1479) Catalonia rose in revolt, and civil war raged for ten years (1462–1472), during which France seized the opportunity to annex Cerdagne and Roussillon. At the end of this exhausting struggle all the fundamental problems remained unsolved, Catalonia had emerged an economic cripple, and public order had largely broken down. Such was the kingdom which Ferdinand inherited in 1479.

Amidst all this, however, there were signs of hope, especially in Castile. Castile was in turmoil, but was showing no signs of exhaustion. The much-maligned Don Álvaro de Luna (d. 1453), finally betrayed to the scaffold by the King whom he had labored faithfully to serve, had appreciated that many of the ills of the land could be remedied by the restoration of a strong central authority, and had done all in his power to attempt to strengthen the hand of John II. Juan de Mena preached the same doctrine in his *Laberinto de Fortuna* (*Labyrinth of Fortune*). The populace knew that something was sadly amiss. There would be, from time to time, a resurgence of optimism. And there were serious, thoughtful, and upright men everywhere, both in the Church and among the nobility, who pondered painfully both on practical politics and on the destiny of Spain.[4]

Juan de Mena was naïve only in imagining that a man as weak-willed and timorous as John II could in any sense "pull himself together" and embark on an energetic, coherent, and ruthless program of reform. He was not wholly wrong to imagine that one charismatic personality, one strong hand invested with the magic aura of monarchy, could work what must have seemed, to all who experienced it, a near-miracle.

II *Isabella*

Volumes have been written on Ferdinand and Isabella, and almost as many again on Isabella herself.[5] Most of them drift into a reverence and enthusiasm which do not help us to determine how much of the transformation which Spain underwent was due to her personally, how much to the political acumen of her husband, how much to obscure social and economic processes, or how much to a simple national psychological reaction against so much that was self-evidently wrong in Spain's immediate unpromising past. Extravagant eulogy still veils the real Isabella (was she really even as beautiful as contemporary writers claim? her portrait painters hardly bear them out); but there can be little doubt that her devoutness, her unswerving rectitude, her energy, her personal courage, her imagination, her single-mindedness and even ruthlessness, all contributed to her success. On the other hand, Castile was more than ready to receive a savior; the anarchically-expended energies of populace and nobility alike needed only to be canalized; and under the direction of Isabella, in a brief thirty years, Spain was transformed. The power and wealth which the Castilian crown had lost or ceded to the great nobility were recovered, and the ambitions of the great were redirected to the service of the state. Law and order were restored in the towns, where municipal government came under the watchful eye of incorruptible royal agents, the *corregidores*. In the countryside the bandits were exterminated by the reorganized Holy Brotherhood, the *Santa Hermandad*. Prosperity returned, along with nascent industry. The administration of justice was purged and speeded up. Printing was introduced, and flourished. Education and learning were fostered, not least by the Queen's own example. In the oft-quoted epigram of the royal chronicler, Juan de Lucena, "When the King gambled, we were all gamblers; but now that the Queen studies, we have all become students."[6] Nomination to the higher offices in the Church became a royal right (conceded by Sixtus IV in 1482), and a new generation of often unwillingly-preferred and puritanically devout men brought about a complete reform of the education and the morals of the clergy. The organization and financing of the army were reviewed; Spanish soldiers learned the new arts of war which were to make them almost invincible for a century; and when the immense host of the Castilian army camped before Málaga (a prize even richer than Granada), it is recorded that there obtained the most perfect discipline: gambling with dice or cards was forbidden by ordinance, blasphemy was prohibited and severely punished, prostitutes could not approach the camp, and scarcely a single brawl occurred.[7] It would be hard to find a more striking contrast with the court of Henry IV.

Spanish arms conquered and absorbed the Muslim Kingdom of Granada, as they were later to annex the Christian Kingdom of Navarre. They were used to phenomenal effect in America, in North Africa, in Italy, and later in Flanders. At the same time the Inquisition was set up to combat heresy, all Jews were expelled from Spain (and subsequently, because of Spanish pressure, from Portugal), and the religious unity of the Peninsula was finally achieved with the expulsion of all the remaining Muslims. For better or for worse, Spain had become, when Isabella died, a monolithic, explosive war machine, powered by new-found prosperity and inspired by nationalistic pride and fanatical crusading zeal.

III   *Spain in Ferment*

The politico-economic transformation which made Spain both the first modern national state and, in the sixteenth century, a world power, was startling. At the same time, not everything in the reign of Isabella was concerned with war, with the politics of power, or with the elimination of dissidence, whether political or religious. It was an age of fecund intellectual ferment also, and the reign of Isabella marks an epoch as memorable in intellectual and literary history as in the political evolution of Europe.

The new humanistic learning from Italy was disseminated at first by private tutors and later by the universities. Feminism never knew a more receptive public in Spain. Poetry never had more practitioners among the grandees. Writers found patrons, and interest and encouragement at the court. They imported new literary forms from abroad—forms, like humanistic comedy, scarcely less important than the meters later imported by Boscán and Garcilaso—and they experimented in a variety of ways.[8] Drama was born, prose fiction took new directions, wit was assiduously cultivated, and the language was revitalized. It is a story which can be read in any history of Spanish literature, even though too many critics and historians, applying anachronistic criteria, find much that was written then to be of inferior quality to what followed in the Golden Age. Isabelline literature is readily conceded to be of great "historical" importance (it would be virtually impossible to deny it that distinction), but it is too rarely, except for *Celestina*, appreciated for its intrinsic merit.

Diego de San Pedro lived through this dramatic and seminal epoch, and was, as we know, encouraged to persist in his literary activities by the ladies of the court, by Doña Marina Manuel, by the Alcaide de los Donceles "and other gentlemen of the court,"[9] and not least by his own master and patron, Don Juan Téllez-Girón. His *Prison of Love*—and one must concede that it is his major work—was read with the greatest avidity, *no tuvo en leerse calma*,[10] but all his writings were known and admired. No writer was ever less conservative. In all he did, he responded instantly, humbly, and perceptively to each new idea and each fresh change of taste or fashion, seeking to please the aristocratic audience whom he alleged to possess discrimination superior to his own; and to look at his works in chronological order is to start to plot a history of taste in the latter part of the fifteenth century and to list the matters—religion, love, politics, courtesy, justice, wit, moral philosophy, literary theory— which preoccupied the minds of men engaged simultaneously in momentous military and political affairs. Just what San Pedro wrote, and how and why he wrote it, will be the subject of the following chapters.

It may be worth observing at this point that I have settled for the not wholly logical label of "an age of transition" in order to avoid fruitless discussion of the problem posed by those who would insist on assigning the reign of Ferdinand and Isabella alternatively to "the Middle Ages," "the Renaissance," or even worse, a "pre-Renaissance."

CHAPTER 3

La Pasión trovada
(The Versified Passion)

I *The Date of* La Pasión trovada

L A PASIÓN TROVADA (*The Versified Passion*) is, as its title indicates, a retelling in verse of the story of the Passion of Christ. It begins with the Agony in the Garden, and ends after the Crucifixion, Deposition, and Burial, before the Resurrection. On more than one occasion its adds matter to the narrative produced by the conflation of the four Gospels, but I leave for the moment the discussion of the nature and significance of these departures from the biblical text. In its final version it consists of 12 plus 236 stanzas of the meter known as *quintillas dobles,* octosyllabic verses arranged in ten-line stanzas with the rhyme-scheme abaab cdccd.

Menéndez Pelayo believed *The Passion* to be the work of San Pedro's extreme old age, principally because it does not figure in San Pedro's catalogue of his "frivolous writings," the works he condemns in the opening stanzas of his *Contempt of Fortune*; but Menéndez Pelayo did not have all the evidence now available to us, and his hypothesis is untenable. *The Versified Passion* was printed several times before *Contempt of Fortune* was written; obviously it would not be included in a catalogue of sinful compositions; San Pedro reused material from it in writing *Las siete angustias de Nuestra Señora (The Seven Sorrows of Our Lady),* which appears as a digression in his first novel, *Arnalte y Lucenda;*[1] the discovery of a MS. version of the poem in an anthology put together in the 1480's reinforces the hypothesis of an early date;[2] and the poem as a whole, though in its printed redaction it reads very smoothly, reveals a relatively unsophisticated versifying technique, far removed

35

from the mastery which San Pedro exhibits in some of his
minor poems, and in *Contempt of Fortune* itself.[3] It is no longer
reasonable to doubt that *The Versified Passion* is an early work,
and, on the evidence we have, almost certainly the earliest
composed of all the works of San Pedro.

II   *The Author of* La Pasión trovada

The circumstances surrounding the composition and subsequent rewriting of San Pedro's *Versified Passion* are still not
entirely clear.[4] The earliest version of it that we possess is in
the MS. "Cancionero de Oñate-Castañeda" (in private hands);
but that version differs in various ways, some extremely important, from the version or versions which found their way into
print. The most notable differences are that it lacks the twelve
introductory stanzas in which the author addresses himself to
a nun with whom he professes to be in love (explaining that
he has put the Passion of Christ into verse in order to forget
his own passion for her), and that it has some sixty additional
stanzas at the end (as well as three extra stanzas in the body
of the text). It is still more disturbing to find that the MS.
attributes the poem to "Pedro de San Pedro," and that the
earlier part of the work, the part which was printed, is conspicuously superior to the ending, which is labored, pedestrian, based
on noncanonical material, and often metrically defective.

There can be no doubt at all that our author was responsible
for the revised version of *The Versified Passion* which was
printed and reprinted from the last decade of the fifteenth
century up to the middle of the nineteenth—printed in the 1850's
not, let it be emphasized, as a medieval work of interest to
scholars, but as a devotional pamphlet which still found popular
appeal. But we cannot be entirely certain that Diego de San
Pedro was responsible for some hypothetical original version of
the poem, now lost. It will no doubt remain forever impossible
to prove, but the facts we have will admit the hypothesis that
the *Passion* was put into verse first by one Pedro de San Pedro
(presumably a relation, and a lamentable rhymester if we can
judge by the ending of the "Oñate-Castañeda" text), and that
this work was largely rewritten and polished by Diego. The

"Oñate-Castañeda" version would represent a halfway stage, a partial revision, in which our author had neither completed the job by refurbishing the last sixty stanzas, nor decided to dispense entirely with the uncanonical and rather tedious matter with which the earliest version ends.[5] (It deals with the confessions of guilt of eight of the disciples.) It could also be assumed to predate the version to which was added the amorous and blasphemous introduction. If "Pedro" is no more than a copyist's slip, we should be driven to conclude that San Pedro's first venture in verse writing, as represented by the final stanzas of the MS., was less than competent—even allowing for the clear evidence of scribal miscopying—and that he made early the most extraordinary progress in facility and felicitousness.

III *Religious Revolution*

San Pedro's *Versified Passion*, if we place the date of its composition before 1480, as it seems we must, is one of the earliest manifestations in Castilian, and certainly the earliest in Castilian verse, of the new religious ideas which elsewhere, in northern Europe, were to lead to Protestantism and the Reformation. In many ways this "revolution" in religious ideas and attitudes—which left its mark equally on Counter-Reformation orthodoxy—was a reactionary movement, in that it was inspired by the old and widely diffused idea of *reformatio* or *renovatio*, of a return to some ideal and idyllic state of primitive and pure Christianity. It is hard to pin it down to one simple formula, but we can easily recognize and point to several of its most characteristic features, all indicative of dissatisfaction with the worldly, ritualistic, and corrupt Church of the later Middle Ages. They include: a renewed interest in the Bible, and most especially the New Testament, with a consequent discarding of apocryphal material and a turning away from much medieval miracle-literature; a shift of emphasis from the person of the Virgin Mother to the person of Christ; an impatience with scholastic theology and an enthusiasm for simple piety; and an insistence on the spiritual life of the individual, on the importance of prayer, and on the *imitatio Christi*, the idea that the life of Christ is the perfect model for that

of the sincere Christian—a concealed corollary of which is the
heretical and rarely-expressed notion that priests and the rites
of the Church are not essential to a man's salvation.[6]

It would be idle to pretend that Diego de San Pedro was
some sort of proto-Protestant, any more than were the members
of the mendicant orders who laid passionate emphasis on "receiving the Word": on heartfelt devotion, genuine contrition,
and sincere piety. And we can see in San Pedro's *Passion* both
the perpetuation of various apocryphal traditions (such as the
earlier life of Judas or the Veronica episode) as well as a strong
devotion to the Virgin. Nevertheless, when we compare San
Pedro's poem with other verse narratives of the life of Christ
composed in the same period, we can perceive some marked
differences. Fray Íñigo de Mendoza wrote (in Spanish) a *Vita
Christi* (which after three thousand lines did not get beyond
the Massacre of the Innocents) in which each episode is glossed
and commented on in the old exegetical tradition, its allegorical
and tropological significance carefully spelled out.[7] Comendador
Román's *Trovas de la gloriosa Pasión* (*Verses on the Glorious
Passion of Our Lord*), as well as his expanded *Coplas de la
Pasión con la Resurrección* (*Verses on the Passion, Together with
the Resurrection*), draw heavily on apocryphal matter. Indeed
the Knight-Commander has only hazy recollections of the
Gospels themselves, for he more than once attributes to Matthew,
say, what is to be found only in Luke or John, and on one
occasion he cites all the Gospels as his authority for something
which is to be found in none of them.[8] Fray Ambrosio de
Montesino's *Coplas sobre diversas devociones y misterios de
nuestra santa fe católica* (*Verses on Various Cults and Mysteries
of Our Holy Catholic Faith*), printed about 1485,[9] is usually
grouped with the other works mentioned, but is fundamentally
different in that it does not offer a consecutive narrative.

Diego de San Pedro does include some apocryphal matter in
his narrative, but it is clear that, although he included them,
he had misgivings even about some long-entrenched apocryphal
traditions, for he fails to mention the names of either Veronica
or Longinus (the blind man cured by the blood from Christ's
side), and he remains, in general, very close to the narrative,
as we shall see.

IV Canonical and Noncanonical Matter

There can be little doubt that, when Diego de San Pedro composed (or revised) *The Versified Passion,* he had the text of the Gospels open before him, for the verbal correspondence between his narrative verses and the biblical narrative is astonishingly close. Given that he was obliged to accommodate his original to rhyming stanzas of ten lines each, the distortion of the words of the Gospels could hardly have been less: he adds only the most innocuous filler-phrases to obtain a rhyme or the requisite number of syllables. Consider (from among hundreds of possible examples) San Pedro's rendering of these well-known lines (I quote alongside the Vulgate text he would have known):

que yo te digo que ante	*dico tibi quia*
qu'esta noche el gallo cante	*in hac nocte antequam gallus*
tres vezes me negarás.	*cantet, ter me negabis.*
Sant Pedro lo que prosigo	*Ait illi Petrus:*
respondió con buena fe:	
Señor, haré lo que digo	
y, si conviene contigo	*Etiamsi oportueret me*
morir, no te negaré.	*mori tecum, non te negabo.*

In the Authorized Version (Matthew 26, 34–35), these two verses are translated as follows (the phrases within square brackets translate the additions which San Pedro was forced to make to meet the requirements of his meter): "Verily I say unto thee, that this night, before the cock crow, thou shalt deny me thrice. Peter [in all good faith] said unto him [the following: Lord, I shall do what I say]; Though I should die with thee, yet I will not deny thee."

These almost literally translated passages form, inevitably, a large part of *The Versified Passion,* and San Pedro (it is unlikely that it was some copyist) took care to mark all such passages with rubrics like *El texto* or *Torna al texto evangelical* ("The author returns to the Gospel text").[10] He was well aware of the distinction between his canonical sources and his other material.

The stanzas in which he departs from and expands the Gospel

narrative can be classified under three broad headings: apocryphal matter, the *Compassio Mariae*, and "meditation" (terms I shall explain). The apocryphal matter proper is of no great importance. The most substantial additions are the allusions to the legendary earlier life of Judas, and the Veronica episode. The story of Judas is included in a highly emotional passage (stanzas 44–52) in which the author turns aside from his story to apostrophize Christ's betrayer. During the Middle Ages Judas was equipped with a biography which borrowed motifs from the story of Moses and the myth of Oedipus (both repeated in sundry other medieval tales): cast adrift on the waters in a basket, he was rescued by a princess, and subsequently, ignorant of his origins, killed his father and married his mother.[11] San Pedro alludes to the murder and incest, crimes and sins of which Christ absolved him, only in order to heighten the accusations of ingratitude which he hurls against him. But he also amplifies his apostrophe with details which fall into other categories: he reproaches Judas with cruel ingratitude to Christ's mother, who so often *made his bed and cooked and served his meals* (stanza 50). This exemplifies the *Compassio Mariae* and "meditation" to which I referred and to which we must return.

The Veronica episode occupies rather more space, and it falls into two parts. In the first part (stanzas 163–64), "a lady" (*una dueña*, unnamed, as I have noted) takes pity on Christ as he begs for a rag to wipe his face, and offers him her wimple. Later (stanzas 192–97), as the Virgin hastens lamenting along the road to Calvary, she is able to show her the face printed in blood and sweat on the cloth, and confirm that the victim is indeed the Virgin's son.[12]

Parts of both these pieces of uncanonical material fall into our second category of intrusions, the *Compassio Mariae*, that is to say, the consequential and simultaneous Passion of Mary.[13] According to the Gospels, Mary plays the most minimal part in the whole story of Christ's Passion, and she is mentioned as being present at the foot of the Cross only by John (19, 25–27), who records the words of Christ, "Woman, behold thy son." But Marian devotion reconstructed for her a much larger, if passive, role: her reactions and laments when St. John and Mary Magdalen bring her the news of Christ's arrest and sentence,

her stumbling, fainting progress along the Via Dolorosa, her
ill-treatment by the populace, her encounter with Veronica, her
first sight of Christ crucified, and so on. It is a supremely
pathetic story, and Diego de San Pedro includes every detail
of it. It must be conceded that at times his devotion to the
Virgin can jar on the modern reader: so, for instance, after
describing in gruesome detail the tortures to which Christ is
subjected, he claims that Mary suffered even more than her
son on learning of them; and there is one singularly tasteless
and obtuse passage (stanzas 212–13) in which he has her railing
at her racked and near-unconscious son for ingratitude, and for
forgetting her anguish in his concern for the salvation of the
human race. But these are rare lapses.

The third way in which San Pedro amplifies the Gospel narrative needs more attention.

V *Meditation*

On numerous occasions Diego de San Pedro includes in his
story matter which is not to be found in the Gospels, but which
cannot properly be labeled "apocryphal." Let us consider just
two examples. Before being crucified, Christ is stripped of his
raiment. Luke and John do not refer to the episode, and both
Matthew (27, 31) and Mark (15, 20) use, in the Vulgate, the
same terse phrase: *induerunt eum vestimentis eius* ("they took
the robe off from him"). And that is all. But in *The Versified
Passion* San Pedro devotes twenty lines to the episode (stanzas
166–67), to remind his readers that Christ had been cruelly
scourged, that the robe they placed upon him was stuck with
his blood to the wounds inflicted on him by the Flagellation,
and that the savage tearing off of his garment reopened those
wounds, causing him great pain, and causing the blood to
flow afresh.

The details of the Crucifixion are even worse. Not one of
the Evangelists describes it in more than two words. In Matthew
(27, 35), Luke (23, 33), and John (19, 18), it is *crucifixerunt eum*
("they crucified him"); in Mark (15, 24) it is *crucifigentes eum*
("when they had crucified him"). Diego de San Pedro expands
this to seventy lines (stanzas 170–76) in order to fill in all the

details. The Gospels provide no clear indication of how the operation was performed, so he opts, first, for the *humi* rather than the *sublime* tradition: that is to say, he has Christ fastened to the cross while it is lying on the ground, and not after it has been erected. We know from another source that Christ was nailed and not tied to it, for John (20, 25) describes the doubting Thomas desiring to place his fingers in the holes caused by the nails. And if there were nails, there must have been hammers. But how far can our imagination go? In San Pedro's version, Christ is laid on the cross to be measured and holes are first drilled in the wood to receive the nails; he is then thrown down again and one hand is fastened with a large, thick nail by merciless hammer-blows; but the executioners, going to fasten the other hand, find that it will not reach the hole that has been drilled to receive the nail, for the agony has caused the muscles of the other arm to contract; they therefore fasten a rope to his wrist and drag on the arm until the hand will reach the hole. . . . And there is yet more of this.

It should be noted at once that very few of the details of this horrifying description were invented by Diego de San Pedro. His source—certainly his ultimate source, through whatever intermediary—is the *Meditationes vitae Christi* (*Meditations on the Life of Christ*), the work of an unknown Franciscan friar of the thirteenth century, although it was until the eighteenth century believed to be the work of St. Bonaventure.[14] This book was one of the most widely known and influential of all religious writings in the later Middle Ages, perhaps not least because, in spite of its inclusion of the *Compassio Mariae* and its "meditative" amplification, it remains wholly faithful to the text of the New Testament, the authentic words of the Bible, for which so many people in Europe had begun to feel a deep hunger. But the *Meditationes* held an even stronger attraction than this, for it offered a guide to a kind of "contemplation" available to everyone.

The anonymous author distinguishes three kinds of Christian life: the active life of good works, the contemplative life, and, third, a second kind of active life, that of the saint who, *vera sapientia imbutus et illuminatus, aliorum salutem intendat* ("who, steeped in and illuminated by true wisdom, sees to the salvation of others"). The contemplative life is similarly divided into three kinds, and the author indicates that he will be concerned only with the simplest and least ambitious of these, *pro incipientis* ("for beginners"). This involves not the contemplation of the majesty of God (this is no mystical treatise) but the *contemplatio humanitatis Christi*, the contemplation of the humanity of Christ, to which any Christian can aspire. The author's premises are quite simply that to know Christ is to love him, that knowledge of Christ purges the Christian of sinful desires, and that the love of Christ is the beginning and the end of all wisdom and virtue. While he is particularly concerned with the elevating effect of contemplating the Passion (*scire Jesum et hunc crucifixum*),[15] he begins in fact from the Nativity.

This technique of "meditation" is of the simplest kind: the reader is urged to consider, contemplate, meditate upon each tiny scrap of information, to reconstruct all the details of the scene, and to let his heart fill with tender and pious devotion. The pseudo-Bonaventure does a good deal of the reader's work for him, but expects him to amplify even further the hints he gives. So, for instance, he devotes a whole chapter (XII) to the Flight into Egypt, which depends ultimately on the most succinct of statements in Matthew (2, 14–15): *Accepit puerem et matrem eius nocte, et secessit in Ægyptum. Et erat ibi usque ad obitum Herodis* ("He took the young child and his mother by night, and departed into Egypt. And was there until the death of Herod"). But what was that journey like? How did the Holy Family support itself in Egypt? The good friar waxes ever more enthusiastic ("What a splendid field for pious and tender meditation!" he exclaims), and his imagination leads him to create a scene in which the child Jesus, taking some piece of sewing to one of his mother's customers, meets with a termagant who takes the work, refuses to pay, speaks harshly to the child, and sends him away without the money. In spite, however, of this abundant detail, our friar ends the chapter saying that he has given his readers no more than a few hints, and that it is for them to fill in the remaining details.

It is the pseudo-Bonaventure who first perceives the horrible consequences of stripping Christ's robe from his scourged and bleeding body: *renovantur fracturae per pannos carni applicatos* ("the wounds are reopened because of the cloth sticking to the flesh"). It is he also who imagines the executioners having to pull on Christ's left arm as they crucify him. It is, however, difficult to point to precise verbal coincidences between San Pedro and the pseudo-Bonaventure, and one can say only that the source of many of San Pedro's details is ultimately the *Meditationes*. It would seem, furthermore, that Diego de San Pedro borrowed not merely some hints but the essential method, for even though the medieval literature on the Passion is so vast that no one could hope to cover it all, there do seem to be details in *The Versified Passion* which have no known antecedents. San Pedro, using the technique of the *Meditationes*, must have invented them for himself.

A further aspect of this method of "meditation" is, of course, the emotive direct address to the reader, urging him to dwell on the horror and cruelty described, to weep, to repent, to be aware of his own inadequacy and sinfulness, to give his heart to Christ. Even without these admonitions, there can be no doubt that *The Versified Passion* makes an impact upon the reader which the terse and unvarnished narrative of the Gospels themselves can fail to do.

Finally, it should be noted that a large proportion of the added matter takes the form of direct speech. A characteristic of all Franciscan preaching (starting with St. Francis himself),[16] a characteristic of the *Meditationes vitae Christi,* and a characteristic of San Pedro's *Versified Passion* is the quantity of material which is presented in the guise of soliloquy or dialogue. There is, indeed, so much direct speech in San Pedro's *Passion* that it furnishes enough for a dramatic representation, and it was actually performed as a play at Lesaca in 1566.[17] (When there exist such obvious antecedents as Franciscan sermons, there is no need, I think, to reconstruct on the evidence of the *Versified Passion* any lost dramatic literature which might have served him, or Fray Íñigo de Mendoza,[18] as a model.)[19]

VI *The Appeal of* The Versified Passion

San Pedro's *Passion* endured as a piece of living devotional literature into the second half of the nineteenth century. It survived a series of mutations and mutilations which, by and large, probably facilitated its acceptance and comprehension by the uneducated. The blasphemous introductory stanzas in which the poet declares his passion for the beautiful nun were not reprinted after about 1530 (and they had been, indeed, deleted from some earlier printings); a continuation of indifferent merit, but which rounded off the somewhat abrupt ending of the printed versions, was composed by a certain *bachiller* Burgos in the eighteenth century and was consistently attached to it thereafter;[20] it lapsed in the sixteenth century into an anonymity which may conceivably have protected it from the seventeenth-century condemnation by the Inquisition of its composer as the author of *Prison of Love;* the *quintillas dobles* (ten-line stanzas) were reprinted as simple *quintillas,* so that half-stanzas containing obscure verses of irremediably archaic syntax and vocabulary could be relatively easily omitted; and from printing to printing, the lexicon, morphology, and syntax were gradually modified and modernized by the ingenuity and often the mere ingenuousness of the compositors, so that if one reads San Pedro's *Passion* in one of its nineteenth-century versions one finds not a single linguistic clue to show that it was originally written four hundred years earlier.

It can scarcely be argued that the popularity of a work of literature depends directly on its literary merit, and the extraordinary success of San Pedro's *Passion* demands explanation in both literary and nonliterary terms. It is absurd to suppose that it owed anything to the popularity of *Prison of Love,* as Michel Darbord suggests,[21] since *The Passion* early fell into anonymity, and it long survived the eclipse of *Prison of Love* which occurred in the seventeenth century. In the same way, Darbord explains nothing when he supposes that it appealed to the taste of fifteenth-century readers. This is not only circular reasoning but does not even approach the problem of its popularity in the centuries after the fifteenth.

Obviously, the success of any best seller depends on many factors which are extraliterary, and this is especially true of a work which lies on the margins between "pure" literature and the kind of didactic, functional literature which may demand some sort of prior assent (in this case, Christian faith) from

its readers. At the same time, when so many other versified
versions of the Passion of Christ failed to achieve the diffusion
or longevity of San Pedro's version, we may be obliged to look
for the key, the factor which tipped the balance, in its aesthetic
merits rather than its devotional content.

As I have indicated, San Pedro's *Versified Passion* was a very
early Spanish response to an emotional need which had been
felt in varying intensity throughout Europe for at least two
hundred years. The religious and moral aspirations of ordinary
people were thwarted in a multiplicity of ways. In the ramified
complexities of the scholastic summations, written of necessity
in Latin, theology had placed itself beyond their comprehension,
and the organized Church had become not the mediating
instrument which it was theoretically supposed to be, but a
barrier not only between the individual layman and the word
of God, the Bible, but also between the individual and God.
The manifest corruption of the higher echelons within the
Church, as well as the ignorance and venality of its lower
representatives, spread cynicism and mistrust, while the Great
Schism dealt a blow to the prestige of the Papacy from which
it took centuries to recover. Natural disasters like the Black
Death were clear evidence of God's displeasure, and the flagrant
contrast between the expressed beliefs and the behavior and
conduct of the great provoked bafflement, resentment, cynicism,
and frustration.

The reaction to the failure of Church and society to live by
the moral norms in which they professed to believe took many
forms. The mendicant orders, especially the early Franciscans
and later the reformed Franciscans of the Observance, preached
poverty and humility, criticized social injustice, fiercely attacked
the iniquities of the nobility and the established Church, and
attempted to invest each action of daily life with moral and
religious significance.[22] Heretical Messianic movements, often
of lunatic complexion, sprang up in every corner of Europe.[23]
Mysticism, the supreme shortcut to God, became a kind of
alternative to intellectualized theology, and faith and not reason
was held by many to be the gateway to understanding: *crede ut
intellegas* ("first believe, and then you will understand") was a
phrase of St. Augustine which was now used as justification

for anti-intellectualism and the dismissal of scholastic subtlety. Antipapal satire, in prose and in verse, proliferated throughout Europe from the twelfth century on.[24] There was an ever-increasing demand for vernacular translations of the Bible, a demand which the Church, not without reason, regarded with alarm. And some serious and devout laymen, like the Brethren of the Common Life, grouped themselves into communities to endeavor to live the true Christian life.[25]

The list of the writings which accompanied this spiritual revolution is enormous—in Latin and in the vernacular languages of Europe, in prose and in verse, in the form of translations, treatises, letters, satires, sermons, dramas, accounts of personal spiritual experiences, and so on. But in the case of the specific form with which we are concerned, a verse narrative of the life of Christ, Castilian has nothing to show before Fray Íñigo de Mendoza's *Vita Christi* and Diego de San Pedro's *Versified Passion*, and these works are considerably later in date than similar works in other major European languages, not excluding Catalan.[26] But San Pedro had a certain advantage in entering late upon the scene, for he did so just as the essential attitudes of the new religious feeling were beginning to crystallize, and, as I have indicated, he showed more sensitivity and discrimination than his Castilian contemporaries in his response to the not wholly articulate spiritual aspirations of the Spanish people.

The introductory stanzas suggest that he wrote *The Passion* at the request of a nun, but we may be allowed to suspect that this is, if not complete fiction, only a half-truth, for it does not seem unreasonable to suppose that this introduction was a later addition, and the idea could well have been prompted by the prologue of the *Meditationes vitae Christi*, which also explains that the book was written for and at the request of a nun—although, of course, the anonymous friar does not profess to be in love with her. But be that as it may, San Pedro clearly had a popular and certainly not highly sophisticated audience in mind. He gave them, as accurately as he could, a translation of the Gospel narratives, avoiding the apocryphal absurdities which abound in Comendador Román's similar work. He incorporated all the detail derived by "meditation" from the canonical text, detail which was absolutely essential to permit the reader to visualize the scene (and which, indeed, Christian iconography had had perforce to reconstruct already).[27] And he showed the way to that simple form of "meditation" whose promised result was compassion, contrition, devotion, and salvation.

At the same time, he did not push his fidelity to the Gospels so far as to exclude material which his readers would have been disturbed to find ignored, such as the role of Mary or the episodes of Veronica or Longinus.[28] Nor did he venture upon the kind of contemporary social criticism in which Fray Íñigo indulged—lively assaults on both individuals and court manners—which resulted first in Fray Íñigo's having to delete certain passages, and, subsequently, in conferring on many of these fascinating fulminations (against indecent dress, cosmetics, jousting, the courtiers' calling one another "cousin" with undue familiarity, etc., etc.) what would be for later generations of little more than historical interest.[29] And he did not venture upon the more abstruse theological themes, such as the allegorical or tropological interpretation of the text, which occupied much of Mendoza's attention. In other words, while San Pedro included what his fifteenth-century audience wanted, he excluded material which would have dated the work for later centuries, and, simultaneously, he avoided excluding material which many medieval extremists would have preferred to omit, and which Counter-Reformation Spain in fact retained in the fabric of its belief.

VII *The Merits of* The Versified Passion

So far, then, we can explain the success of *The Passion* in largely extraliterary terms. Indeed, if one thinks only in terms of literary merit, it would be impossible to explain why the initially very popular *Vita Christi* of Mendoza did not enjoy a success as long-lived as San Pedro's. But *The Versified Passion* does also possess considerable literary merit and shows a superb adaptation of style to purpose in the simplicity of its diction, in its smooth versification, in its dramatic presentation of lively imagined dialogue, and in the tremendous emotional effects produced by the vividness of its re-creation of events and the author's intervention in compelling exclamatory appeals to his readers. Without extensive quotation in Spanish it is difficult to illustrate these qualities. Moreover, quotation out of context cannot properly convey the shock, the enormous emotional impact, which San Pedro repeatedly achieves with verses of the utmost simplicity. Nevertheless, it may be worth attempting to analyze just one of a large number of possible examples.

St. John and Mary Magdalen bring to the Virgin the news of the torture and imminent crucifixion of Christ (stanzas 180–83). Mary faints on hearing this but recovers and, without pausing to dress properly, rushes into the street in a cold sweat and beside herself with anguish (stanza 186). Her tears, her wild actions, her inarticulate despair, are described in two more stanzas (187–88). Then in her grief she addresses the bystanders, the women she meets, appealing to all those who have been mothers, to all those who know what it is to lose a husband, to all who have ever loved someone: *llorad comigo mi mal* ("weep with me in my misfortune"), and the stanza (189) closes with her explanation: *que le están dando la muerte / a un hijo que yo tenía* ("they are putting to death a son I once had").

The phraseology could hardly be simpler, and a close reading of these words could easily lead us into hypersubtlety. And yet there *are* other ways in which it might have been put, and in context it does have the jolting effect to which I referred. The initial colloquial *que* is the all-purpose conjunction of popular speech, and cannot be properly translated by the literary English "for" or "because." The impersonal third-person plural of the verb conjures up not the specific, the hostile Jews or Roman soldiers, but "Them," the unreasonable, unfeeling, and inimical forces of authority before which we are helpless. The Spanish continuous construction of *estar* with the gerundive emphasizes, more than the English can, the duration and continuity of the process: it is not a swift and merciful death but death by inches; it is not a perfect tense, when the only reaction could be grief and ultimately resignation, but a present process demanding immediate desperate action, a flight through the streets of a crowded city, a fight against time, to reach him before he dies. It is not "my son"; it is not "the Son of God"; it is "a son," a conceptualization deprived of a possessive which equates Mary with all the other mothers who have ever lived.

Que yo tenía is a past imperfect tense, not the simple present: the Virgin is already anticipating that future in which she will be able to refer to Christ only as the son which she used to have.

Now it may well be that Diego de San Pedro did not really have all this in mind when he penned those two verses. But there are literary effects of which he was undoubtedly wholly conscious. He was certainly fully cognizant of the effects to be obtained from a structured context. He builds up to these two lines with some care, as Mary moves from shock and unconsciousness, through wild and desperate action (tearing her hair, falling on her knees to kiss the trail of bloodstains), through the barely coherent articulation of her grief and despair, addressing in exclamations of anguish any strangers who will listen, to the point at which she is able to formulate for them the simple explanation of the cause of her distress. The simplicity and brevity of her words and the transition from incoherence to articulate expression produce a climax of supreme pathos which was quite clearly deliberately engineered.

Furthermore, it is obvious that San Pedro was fully aware of the relative importance of the position of the verses within his ten-line stanzas, for repeatedly he places the most significant of his phrases at the end of a stanza and at the conclusion of a syntactical period. That this is more than the subjective impression of one reader can readily be demonstrated, I believe, by looking at San Pedro's positioning in his poem of the most pregnant phrases of the Gospel narrative: "Watch and pray, that ye enter not into temptation" (stanza 14; Matthew 26, 41; Mark 14, 38); "O my Father, if it be possible, let this cup pass from me" (stanza 19; Matthew 26, 39; Mark 14, 36; Luke 22, 42); "I shall smite the shepherd, and the sheep shall be scattered abroad" (stanza 24; Matthew 26, 31; Mark 14, 27); "Though I should die with thee, yet will I not deny thee" (stanza 26; Matthew 26, 35; Mark 14, 31); or, so as not unduly to extend what could easily be a very long list of quotations and references, "All they that take the sword shall perish by the sword," "And immediately the cock crew," "They said, Barrabas," "Father, forgive them; for they know.not what they do," "Lord, remember me when thou comest into thy kingdom," "My God, my God, why hast thou forsaken me?", "He said, It is finished."

As I have indicated, quotation out of context cannot begin to convey the impact which such phrases have in a structured context, and the factors which contribute to their climactic effect in the narrative are many and varied: though put into octosyllabic rhyming verse, the familiar phrases are beautifully and naturally translated, and are instantly recognizable by readers who know only the Authorized Version and have never looked at a Spanish Bible or the Vulgate text; and these familiar words are spaced out, isolated, so that one phrase does not follow hard upon another, to diminish its effect; they are, moreover, thrown into relief by their position at the ends of stanzas. The very amplification of San Pedro's account of the Passion serves, therefore, to bring out the precise effects which a reader could achieve, if he would, by "meditation."

In many late medieval sermons one senses a kind of frustrated desperation in the preacher: his congregation is sitting listening to his words and presumably understanding what he is saying, but they are not really taking it to heart, they will forget what he has said as they go out through the church door, they have *heard* the Word but they have not *received* it. Diego de San Pedro has in *The Versified Passion* contrived to make this kind of indifference virtually impossible. He assaults the reader's sensibilities in a hundred ways. The familiarity which breeds indifference is stripped from a familiar narrative, and the familiar Gospel phrases are forced into relief; the full horror of that series of atrocities is hammered home; there is an immediacy in the vividness with which scenes and dialogue are reconstructed; there is tension in the way the slow but relentless progression of events carries the reader compulsively forward; and the author is ever present, insistent, demanding attention, working on the reader's emotions. The *intensity* of *The Passion* is one of its most conspicuous features, and is something of which various modern critics appear to have remained inexplicably unaware.

VIII   *Criticism of* The Versified Passion

Hostile criticism of San Pedro's *Passion* falls into two quite distinct categories. In one camp are those critics who have

dismissed it as doggerel. The earliest of these, though to quote
him out of context is to misquote him,[30] was Jerónimo Arbolanche, who wrote: "I do not know how to compose *The Passion*
as Diego de San Pedro did, nor, later, *Prison of Love*, for the
one resembles a blind man's recitation, and the other a tale
for gravediggers."[31] It is invariably forgotten that Arbolanche,
in his extraordinary initial verses, also writes derogatorily of
Anacreon, Pindar, Plautus, Sappho, Euripides, Menander, Virgil,
Ovid, Horace, Terence, Lucan, Dante, Petrarch, Ariosto, Mena,
Santillana, Torres Naharro, Boscán, Montemayor, and many
more of only slightly less repute. But Menéndez Pelayo seems
to echo Arbolanche's phrases when he terms it "facile and
feeble" (*coplas fáciles pero algo lánguidas*), and says, "The
general tone of the composition, and even the meter, seem
designed for recitation by blind beggars in the street";[32] while
Gili Gaya omits *The Passion* from his edition of the works of
San Pedro on the grounds that "this work of a vulgar rhymester
lacks literary merit" and that it could hold no appeal for modern
readers.[33] It is true that neither Menéndez Pelayo nor Gili Gaya
had access to any of the fifteenth- or sixteenth-century editions
of the poem, but Michel Darbord arrives at similar conclusions
on the basis of at least one of the early editions. As for certain
other historians of Spanish literature, one suspects that they
really knew no more about the work than what they had read
in Menéndez Pelayo. The fact that Quevedo, in the *Visita de los
chistes*, places in the mouth of Pero Grullo (who speaks only in
clichés) two verses from the opening of the poem could well
be interpreted as testimony to the diffusion of the work rather
than as an equation of San Pedro with Pero Grullo. In any event,
these dismissive judgments cannot stand. As his other verse
demonstrates, Diego de San Pedro was much more than a facile
rhymester; he was responsible, as we shall see, for some of the
most ingenious and concentrated verse extant in Spanish; and
the ease with which he varied his prose style shows that if
The Passion is "simple" it is because he chose to make it so.

Its apparent simplicity is also misleading. While the syntax
is natural and unforced, and the vocabulary consists of words
of high frequency, the language is by no means free from
rhetorical devices of the more emotive varieties (exclamations,

rhetorical questions, various forms of repetition) nor, as Dorothy Severin has shown, from the less elaborate types of conceit which stud contemporary amorous poetry. Moreover, in this poem of almost twenty-five hundred lines it is less the detail than the large effect which is important, and there can be little doubt, as I have tried to show, that San Pedro studied carefully the ways in which he could build his verses to a series of climaxes and achieve the maximum impact upon his audience. It is most certainly not the work of a *coplero vulgar*, a mere poetaster. Nor is it in any sense "feeble."

But the other criticism is one that cannot easily be swept aside, even if it does not reflect upon San Pedro's ability as an artist. The heterodox Spanish humanist Juan de Valdés attacked the very concept of this kind of "meditation" in his *Diálogo de la doctrina cristiana* (*Dialogue on Christian Doctrine*): "those imaginings that some take to be 'contemplation'— I do not know what they are, nor what profit anyone can derive from them."[34] He denies, in fact, that the imaginative reconstruction of concrete reality can have any value as a spiritual exercise. Eventually, of course, we are led into a theological problem, for Valdés believed emphatically that simply reading the Scriptures, or even pondering upon the words of the Bible, was very far from being a sure recipe for virtue or salvation, and insisted that only God's grace could give spiritual inspiration to sinful Man. The orthodox Church of the Counter-Reformation agreed with neither Valdés nor the naïve pseudo-Bonaventure. It had seen the disastrous consequences of letting the Scriptures fall into the hands of those who felt entitled to interpret them as they would, and it was not prepared to tolerate the vagaries of belief which might be dictated by individual conscience.

The criticism of Valdés does, however, raise a serious and fundamental problem. Was what San Pedro set out to achieve worth achieving? This question also suggests itself in a slightly different form if one looks at another versified Passion, *La Cristiada* (*The Epic of Christ*) by Fray Diego de Hojeda, printed in 1611.[35] This work, more readily comparable with *Paradise Lost* than with *The Versified Passion*, is altogether grander in conception; it sets the Passion of Christ in the context of world history; and, since the Crucifixion is represented as the final victory over the Devil and the hosts of Hell, the whole poem is filled with light and optimism. (It must be noted, however, that for reasons not easy to understand, it fell on barren ground and was never reprinted.) When one contrasts the two works, one becomes aware of the narrowness of San Pedro's vision, of the gloom, gore, and anguish in which the poem is steeped, and, most notably, of the disturbing way in which the poet dwells on the hideous details of the physical sufferings of Christ and the sadistic indignities to which he is subjected. One begins to suspect that there may be something profoundly unhealthy about this concentration on this one episode and in the total omission not only of all that preceded it, but also of the Resurrection. Repeatedly San Pedro insists that we should weep and wail; *¡cristianos, llorad, gemid!, sospiremos y lloremos, ¡O quién gemiese y llorasse!*, etc. It is a form of Christian meditation which makes only the most token and perfunctory reference to the Good News. If this is what the fifteenth-century readers wanted, is it what they ought to have had? Just what benefit did they derive from this limited contemplation of the humanity of Christ?

One might say that the poem belongs to an age of fanaticism, but Mendoza's *Vita Christi,* from the same period, makes much more cheerful reading. The real answer seems to be that both the positive literary merits and the possible fundamental defects of *The Versified Passion* are reflections of the personality of the author. Diego de San Pedro was ever a purist, a perfectionist, and an extremist, wholly dedicated to giving his audience precisely what it demanded. He lacked, perhaps, the moral independence which would have allowed him to go his own way, unheeding of success or blame. If, therefore, one thinks to impute the tone and attitudes of *The Passion* to that chaotic period of political and spiritual turmoil before the Isabelline peace, one must also take account of the other half of the combination: *The Passion* is the product of author plus environment.

CHAPTER 4

Las siete angustias de Nuestra Señora (The Seven Sorrows of Our Lady)

I *The Genre*

THE history of the literary genre to which we must assign Diego de San Pedro's poem on *The Seven Sorrows* (or *Dolors*) *of Our Lady* begins in the twelfth century, in medieval Latin,[1] and makes its earliest appearance in Spanish in the thirteenth century, in the first of the *cantigas,* or songs, which Alfonso X (1252–1284) dedicated to the Virgin, celebrating her *VII goyos* (her "Seven Joys").[2] It must be noted, however, that not only do the Seven Joys antedate by a considerable margin of time the Seven Sorrows, but that almost two centuries elapsed before the figure of seven became consecrated as the standard number of Joys or Sorrows (matching, of course, such series as the seven deadly sins, the seven virtues, the seven "words" of Christ on the Cross, etc.). There are lyric poems on the Joys of the Virgin composed by the Archpriest of Hita, by an anonymous poet in the *Cancionero de Baena,*[3] by Fernán Pérez de Guzmán, by the Marquis of Santillana, and various others. The number of Joys is far from uniform and there are poems which celebrate five, nine, twelve, and even fifteen Joys. That by Santillana lists twelve, and makes use (actually quoting and weaving into the poem the Latin words) of the famous hymn composed by St. Thomas à Becket, *Gaude, Virgo, Mater Christi.*

It was some time before the parallel series of Sorrows appeared, and at first we find no more than odd poems dedicated to individual episodes. Again the earliest Spanish poet in the field is King Alfonso X, in one of whose *cantigas* there appears the image of the sword which (metaphorically) pierced Mary's heart; and once more the origin of the image is to be found in medieval Latin, probably in the superb hymn *Stabat Mater,* in which there occur the lines: *cujus animam gementem / contristatam* [or *contristantem*] *et dolentem / pertransivit gladius* ("whose wailing, anguished, grieving heart was pierced as by a sword").[4]

The Church eventually established the feast of the Seven Sorrows, or the Seven Swords or Knives (*septem gladii*), in 1423; but there was still no general agreement about precisely which of the many moments of anguish in the life of the Virgin were to be recognized as the consecrated Seven, and while poets continued to compose verses on one or other of the individual Sorrows, the first poet in Spanish to treat of all seven was either Diego de San Pedro or Gómez Manrique.[5] Neither of the pieces composed by these two poets can be dated with sufficient accuracy to determine which came first. (It would be reasonable to date San Pedro's poem *c.* 1480, but Gómez Manrique's cannot be pinned down nearly so narrowly.)

Gómez Manrique's poem, much shorter than San Pedro's, is entitled *Los cuchillos del dolor de Nuestra Señora* (*The Knives of Sorrow of Our Lady*) and selects the following seven episodes in the Virgin's life: (1) the prophecy of Simeon; (2) the flight into Egypt; (3) the Child lost in the Temple; (4) the arrest and trial of Christ; (5) the Crucifixion; (6) the Descent from the Cross; and (7) the Burial. These do not agree with San Pedro's seven, which are: (1) the same: the prophecy of Simeon; (2) the Child lost in the Temple (Gómez Manrique's third); (3) the news of the Crucifixion brought by St. John and Mary Magdalen; (4) the sight of Christ on the Cross; (5) the Descent from the Cross (the Pietà of so much Renaissance painting and sculpture), which is Gómez Manrique's sixth Sorrow; (6) the Burial; and (7) Mary's parting from the corpse and tomb of her son, and returning to her house.

II *The Relationship of* The Seven Sorrows *and* The Passion

It will be noted that of San Pedro's series of Seven Sorrows, five are associated with the Passion (and *Compassio Mariae*). The MS. version of *The Versified Passion* in Oñate-Castañeda deals at length with three of them (omitting the last two), while the printed versions deal with two (omitting also Mary's lament as she holds the dead Christ in her arms). But when we look at the two poems we find that we have to do with more than a simple coincidence of topics or verbal reminiscences: whole stanzas from *The Passion* are taken over word for word— there are eleven *quintillas* in this category—and a further six half-stanzas coincide except for a change from third to second person.[6] (Instead of narrating the events in the third person as he does in *The Passion*, San Pedro apostrophizes the Virgin: it is "you fainted" and not "she fainted".) There can be little doubt that San Pedro wrote (or rewrote) *The Passion* before he composed *The Seven Sorrows*.[7] The textual indications, when viewed individually, may be regarded as slight, but cumulatively they are decisive.

The crux of the argument is that when one looks at the stanzas which are common to both works, one perceives that on several occasions phrases which are perfectly in place in *The Versified Passion* are, mildly if never very seriously, anomalous in the context of *The Seven Sorrows*. I shall cite only one example, not as proof of the proposition, but as an indication of the way in which the proposition can be justified.

In *The Passion* (stanzas 180–81) St. John arrives bringing to Mary the news of Christ's imminent crucifixion; he has barely finished speaking (*Sant Juan no bien acabando / de recontalle su pena*, stanza 182) when Mary Magdalen enters, in a delirium of anguish and tearing out her hair by the handful (*sacando con ravia esquiva / sus cabellos a manojos*), to tell the Virgin that Christ has been crucified and is dying. Now in San Pedro's version of *The Seven Sorrows of Our Lady*, the news of the Crucifixion constitutes only one Sorrow, and the poet telescopes the scene by having St. John and Mary Magdalen come in together and begin to relate, in chorus, the account which in *The Passion* is given to Mary Magdalen alone. But in borrowing these verses ready-made from *The Passion*, the poet included one anomalous detail and neglected to make one necessary change.

First of all, he uses the lines *sacando con ravia esquiva / sus cabellos a manojos* with reference to both Mary Magdalen and

St. John. While this is no doubt far from decisive, it does seem that the gesture of tearing out handfuls of hair is on the whole appropriate for Mary Magdalen, but less so for St. John. More convincing, perhaps, is the second anomaly: San Pedro has turned Mary Magdalen's narrative lament into a duet, recited by her and St. John, and he therefore makes the appropriate changes in the number of the verb *in the first quintilla*, so that the *segund yo lo vi tratar* ("to judge from the way I saw him being treated") of *The Passion* becomes, naturally enough, *según lo vimos tratar* ("to judge from the way *we* saw him being treated") in *The Seven Sorrows*. But in the next *quintilla*, in which the account is continued, the words are identical with those used in *The Passion*, and the first-person verbs are in the singular. In other words, the author has reverted to his conception of the speech as a monologue by Mary Magdalen, and has simply copied the verses from *The Passion*, either forgetting that both St. John and Mary Magdalen are speaking, or simply finding it too difficult to accommodate, without extensive rewriting, the extra syllables necessary to pluralize the verbs.

We must suppose, therefore, that after completing the first long narrative poem in Spanish on the Passion of Christ, Diego de San Pedro thought to introduce a further novelty into Castilian literature: a substantial poem on the Seven Sorrows of Mary.[8] The pattern which imposed itself was a simple one, and was probably suggested by the method he had already used in *The Passion*: first, a simple narrative statement about the event in question (sometimes amplified by imagined dialogue as in the case of the news of the Crucifixion), then the Virgin's lament, and finally the poet's emotive expressions of compassion and shared anguish. Part of the necessary material, rather more, in fact, than the seventeen *quintillas* which he borrowed, already existed in *The Passion*, and San Pedro chose the best of these stanzas and completed the work by composing the necessary additional material.

One further curious detail is worth noting, and that is the coincidence of the initial verse of San Pedro's poem with that of a *cantiga* in praise of the Virgin composed by Alfonso Álvarez de Villasandino earlier in the century, *Virgen digna de alabança* ("O Virgin, worthy of the highest praise").[9] Villasandino had

claimed that that poem alone would suffice to save him from Hell
(from *el Enemigo*, the Devil), and we may imagine that in
borrowing that initial line San Pedro was quite deliberately chal-
lenging comparison with Villasandino, and, indeed, inviting his
readers to admit that he had actually surpassed the older poet.

III   The Seven Sorrows *and* Arnalte y Lucenda

What precisely happened thereafter is by no means clear.
What we know of the printing history of *The Seven Sorrows* is
as follows: the earliest extant printing of the poem is the
version contained in the first known edition of *Arnalte and
Lucenda*, done in Burgos in 1491.[10] There the lovelorn and
rejected Arnalte, toward the end of the novel, composes and
recites *The Seven Sorrows of Our Lady* to try to forget his
own sorrows—much as Diego de San Pedro himself claimed to
have composed *The Passion* in order to assuage his own passion
for the nun. The next known, but no longer extant, printing
was that done by Hurus in Zaragoza in 1492 in a religious
anthology, which was reprinted in 1495.[11] There the poem has
two extra stanzas, to be found within the body of the poem.[12]
The next extant edition of *Arnalte*, of Burgos, 1522, does not
contain *The Seven Sorrows* and the prose context of the poem
is rewritten so that the excision of these stanzas is not made
evident.[13] Although there must have been various independent
editions of the poem in *pliegos sueltos*, or chapbooks, the first
of which we have any information is one done in Medina del
Campo in 1534, now lost;[14] and the earliest extant *pliego* of
The Seven Sorrows is to be dated around 1550.[15]

It is obvious from an inspection of the texts that the earliest
printed version, that contained in the *Arnalte* of 1491, is not the
source of the version of the Hurus *cancionero* or of the later
pliego suelto. Moreover, this pious digression does not really
seem appropriate in the tale of the love of Arnalte for Lucenda,
and it was excised from the edition of 1522. The problem is to
know whether the first printing of the poem (an edition now
perhaps lost) was as an independent work, or as a digression
within *Arnalte and Lucenda*. And it would also be useful to
know whether San Pedro composed the poem independently, or
specifically for inclusion in his first novel.

It is not possible to give firm answers to these questions, and it is not easy to attempt to assess the probabilities of the different solutions. Despite the resemblance between the reasons given by San Pedro and Arnalte for composing religious verse— *The Passion* and *The Seven Sorrows* respectively—it may be thought unlikely that the author, in the course of writing *Arnalte and Lucenda,* would turn aside to compose a poem of this length, written in a totally different vein from the novel. There are, however, some considerations which do not make this entirely improbable. Within the novel, *The Seven Sorrows* forms a symmetrical pair with a long poem in praise of Queen Isabella, which is placed near the beginning of the story; and Regula Langbehn-Rohland has suggested that neither poem is alien to the theme of the love story, in that the subject of each is, in different ways, an example of the perfect woman.[16] I am inclined to suspect, however, that even if *The Seven Sorrows* was first printed in an early and now lost edition of *Arnalte and Lucenda,* San Pedro must have composed it earlier, and seized on a somewhat slender pretext to insert it and print it in the novel.

It is also tempting to suppose that San Pedro wrote *The Seven Sorrows* before the revised and shortened version of *The Versified Passion* appeared in print. The abbreviation of the ending of *The Passion,* in which the last three of the Sorrows appear only as brief narrative, without the Virgin's laments, could be explained by the fact that San Pedro had treated them at length in *The Seven Sorrows.*

The Seven Sorrows of Our Lady does not show to best advantage in the context in which it is habitually read, that is, in the story of *Arnalte and Lucenda.* There it smacks of blasphemy, it has virtually nothing to do with the story, it demands a radical switch of perspective from the reader, it has the effect of making Arnalte's misfortunes look trivial, and it holds up tediously and not suspensefully the *dénouement* of the whole novel. It demands to be read as the independent poem which it became, even if it did not begin its life in that way. When looked at quite separately, it is found to have some of the best qualities of *The Versified Passion*: simplicity and emotional force. At the same time, it lacks some of the more jarring features of *The Passion,* such as the gruesome details of the tortures, or the ferocious, near-hysterical diatribes against the Jews. Its curious dual relationship with *The Passion* on the one hand and *Arnalte and Lucenda* on the other has perhaps obscured for critics its own particular merits; and its innovatory nature has never been recognized by historians. It is still to be placed in its proper position, of both priority and merit, in the history of Spanish literature.

CHAPTER 5

Arnalte y Lucenda (Arnalte and Lucenda)

I *The Story*

*A*RNALTE y *Lucenda*, or, to give it its full title, *Tratado de amores de Arnalte y Lucenda* (*The Story of the Loves of Arnalte and Lucenda*),[1] was Diego de San Pedro's first essay in writing prose fiction, and must have been completed about 1481.[2] Addressed to the ladies of the Queen, it tells the story of the endeavors of the luckless hero, Arnalte, to win the hand of Lucenda.

Like several other "sentimental novels" (an ill-defined genre which I discuss below), it is told in the first person (by the Author, and then by Arnalte), and, like *El siervo libre de amor* (*The Free Slave of Love*) of Juan Rodríguez del Padrón or *Proceso de cartas* (*Exchange of Letters*) of Juan de Segura, it consists structurally of a tale within a tale.

The action opens when the narrator, a long way from Castile, finds himself lost in the wilderness just as the sun is setting. Seeing the smoke of a habitation, he makes for the place and finds a strange, black palace populated by men dressed in mourning. Received by their pale and sighing lord, he is courteously treated and given supper and a bed, but cannot sleep for the noise of wailing, lamentation, and doleful music. In the morning he is taken to mass in the private chapel and sees a tomb already prepared with its epitaph: "You see before you the monument of a wretched man whose complaint is that he and she do not lie in it together" (*Vedes aquí la memoria / del triste que se querella / porque no están él y ella*). After breakfast the narrator and his host engage in conversation. The melancholy knight (it is Arnalte, but he has not yet revealed his name) tells the narrator that he knows King Ferdinand (*al Rey nuestro señor conoscía*) and inquires whether this great man

62

has a Queen worthy of him. The author, keenly conscious of
the inadequacy of his talent, then launches into a poem of 210
lines in praise of Isabella. At its conclusion, his host, now confident of our author's discretion and good sense, makes him
promise to recount his story to all women of sense and sensibility (*mugeres no menos sentidas que discretas*) and begins
his tale. From this point to the end of the novel, when the
narrator addresses himself to the ladies of the court, we have
only Arnalte's story, with no intervention from the narrator, a
structure which contrasts, as we shall see, with that of *Prison
of Love*.

Arnalte, then, is a noble native of Thebes, brought up at
the court of its king. But attending one day the funeral of a
great lord, he sees the nobleman's distressed and weeping
daughter, Lucenda, and forthwith falls in love with her. We
are then given a lengthy account of the sundry stratagems by
which Arnalte attempts to establish contact with Lucenda:
first he writes her a letter (the text of which we are given
verbatim), which he has his page deliver and which Lucenda
tears up on the spot; he then disguises himself as a woman,
places himself next to Lucenda in church on Christmas morning,
and makes her a long speech (quoted in full) but she rejects
his advances and orders him to cease molesting her (speech);
he then composes a serenade which he has sung outside her
window, again without result, and he laments his misfortune
(soliloquy); at a tournament before the King and Queen, Arnalte
carries an ingenious device to make Lucenda aware that his
passion persists; at the ball on the evening of the tournament
Arnalte (wearing yet another device) persuades Lucenda to
dance with him, and, while she is standing next to the Queen
and cannot make any protest, pushes a letter (given verbatim)
into her pocket—a letter which his page, sent the following
morning to check the rubbish thrown from Lucenda's house,
cannot discover.

Other characters are then brought into the plot. Arnalte's
sister Belisa is worried about him and begs him to confide in
her (speech), but Arnalte refuses to tell her what is wrong
(speech). He thinks instead of his friend Elierso, whose house
is next to Lucenda's, reveals to him his love for her, and begs

to be allowed to watch her from Elierso's windows (speech).
Elierso confesses that he is himself in love with Lucenda, but
he places their close friendship first and agrees to help Arnalte
in any way he can (speech). Arnalte is at once suspicious and
jealous, but conceals his feelings and begins to frequent Elierso's
house in the hope—the vain hope as it turns out—of seeing
Lucenda. Meanwhile Belisa, who is a close friend of Lucenda,
becomes convinced that her brother is in love with her friend,
and appeals to Lucenda on his behalf (speech). Lucenda, however, refuses her (speech). Arnalte thinks that Lucenda may
be moved if he pretends to forget her, convinces his sister that
he intends to go into exile, and Belisa finally secures (speeches
from Belisa and Lucenda) a grudging letter from Lucenda
(given in full) in which she makes it clear that she thinks his
self-exile is a deception. Arnalte replies by letter (given in
full) and Belisa arranges a rendezvous for him with Lucenda,
in the chapel of a convent, with herself as chaperone. At this
interview, Lucenda laments her indiscretion in agreeing to it,
and permits him to kiss her hand, on condition that he importune
her no further (speech).

Arnalte is overjoyed, but by now so broken in health that he
allows Belisa to persuade him to take a hunting holiday on her
estate, to recover his strength. But sundry bad omens remind
him of his suspicions of Elierso, who has been avoiding him for
some time. He climbs a hill not far from Thebes to see if he can
descry Lucenda's house, and the noise of drums and trumpets
reaches his ears. Perturbed, he returns at nightfall to his sister's
country house to find her silent and in tears: Elierso and Lucenda
are married, and Arnalte falls in a deathlike faint.

Incensed by this treachery, Arnalte challenges Elierso to
a duel (letter of challenge given verbatim). Elierso replies, also
by letter, alleging that he has taken Lucenda as his wife not
for his own benefit, but in order to cure his friend of his passion.
But since Arnalte has now publicly dishonored him by his
accusations, he chooses the weapons (horses, armor, lances, and
swords). The King, disgusted by Elierso's behavior, agrees to
supervise the duel and guarantee obedience to the rules. In the
fight Elierso is finally beaten, "by which his treachery and the
justice of my cause were demonstrated" (*en el cual vencimiento*

su falsedad y mi verdad se conosció), but he refuses to admit
his guilt and Arnalte kills him.

While Arnalte, at home, is recovering from his wounds, he
learns of Lucenda's grief and decides to write to her, offering
himself in Elierso's place as her husband (*de escrevirle acordé
ofreciéndome por su marido*). Belisa duly carries his letter
(quoted in full) to Lucenda, and communicates to her the offer
of marriage. Lucenda makes no reply, but proceeds with her
household to a convent of the strictest discipline, and takes her
vows. When Belisa attempts to speak further with her, Lucenda
has the abbess send her away. Arnalte, now that every remedy
has failed, attempts to assuage his sorrow by reciting *The Seven
Sorrows of Our Lady,* but to no avail. He decides, therefore, to
withdraw to the wilderness. His sister tries to dissuade him
(speech), but he is determined on this course (speech). He
vaits only long enough to have the King find a husband for his
sister and to attend her marriage. He then departs with his
household for the place where the author has found him, and
he ends his story repeating his request to the author to recount
his misfortunes to compassionate ladies.

In a brief *envoi,* the author addresses the ladies of the court,
apologizing for the inadequacies of his narration, and asking
them to bear in mind that his only purpose was to entertain them.

II *Narrative and Discourse*

Before considering some of the more general problems which
are presented by this story, there is one major point which needs
to be emphasized: and that is, that while there is in the tale of
Arnalte and Lucenda a good deal of incident, primarily in the
nonstructural complication of the plot (such as the various
unsuccessful stratagems employed by Arnalte to approach Lucenda), the plot is not the most important part of the novel.
The "external" plot is carried forward for the most part by
comparatively brief narrative units, and for some parts of the
tale Diego de San Pedro takes very little more space than I
have devoted to summarizing them. In fact, in terms of the
sheer number of pages devoted to them, the linking narrative
"chapters" actually occupy fewer than the set pieces, the letters,

and speeches whose existence I indicated in the synopsis of the story. And the most important constituent of the novel is precisely these set pieces, which cannot be summarized nearly so easily as the "external" plot.

Even if they cannot be kept entirely separate, it is possible to distinguish two levels of action in *Arnalte and Lucenda*. On the one hand, we have the "external" plot of mere physical events: "Arnalte meets Lucenda and talks to her; Lucenda replies; Arnalte returns home"; and on the other hand, we have the "internal" plot of the arguments employed by the participants, of their statements about their feelings, of their reactions to the statements made and the arguments adopted by the other, and so forth.

The units which are by far the most important for carrying this "internal" plot are the speeches and letters (rhetorically indistinguishable in structure). Each is a most carefully constructed and beautifully written piece, which analyzes minutely the sentimental situation, advances ingenious and persuasive (if sometimes specious) arguments, and almost invariably describes in detail the psychological state of the writer or the speaker. It is, as we shall see, this analysis of passion, this close scrutiny of the nature, the effects, and the metaphysics of love, which is new in Castilian prose, and which is the mark of the "sentimental novel" as it was conceived by Diego de San Pedro.

The quite invariable separation, into what we should nowadays tend to call "chapters," of the direct speech of the characters and the indirect speech or narrative attributed to "the Author" by the "chapter headings," the rubrics, is something that usually strikes modern readers as strange and even artificial. It is not a mode of narration to which modern novels have habituated them; they expect narration and "dialogue" to be interwoven. As one modern critic complained of *Prison of Love,* "the characters live in perpetual monologue."[3]

It is certainly true that one will look in vain, in both *Arnalte and Lucenda* and *Prison of Love,* for anything like the dialogue of a modern novel. Occasionally San Pedro reports in very summary terms a conversation necessary to the advancement of the "external" plot—such as Belisa's informing him that Lucenda is married, his telling the King of Elierso's treachery, his arranging for Belisa's marriage, and so on. These exchanges, however, are never given in direct speech, but form part of a narrative unit. The "dialogue" which *is* reported at length, and in direct speech, consists usually of a pair of monologues. One of the interlocutors states uninterruptedly and in detail his or her petition,[4] and the other replies, answering the argument point by point. The speeches, in fact, in rhetorical structure, in length, and in function, are quite indistinguishable from the letters. The characters speak to each other just as though they were writing letters. The procedure is one which demands both explanation and justification.

The explanation is a comparatively simple one: Diego de San Pedro is following quite scrupulously the dictates of late classical and medieval rhetorical theory.[5] For the medieval theorists—and their dependence on and elaboration of such works as the anonymous pseudo-Ciceronian *Rhetorica ad Herennium* need not detain us here—dialogue, *colloquia personarum*, is the mode of presentation of a conversation which characterizes drama. (And, incidentally, it may be worth pointing out that the dialogue of the drama of the period is also "artificial," in as much as matter which might more realistically be conveyed by the narrative intervention of the author has to be presented through the mouths of the characters: description of other characters, description of the setting, reactions concealed from the other characters but revealed to the audience by means of asides, internal musings externalized in soliloquies, and so forth.)

The theorists are prepared to accept some minimal dialogue in narrative, *narratio*, but they would prefer to restrict it to certain types of *narratio*, namely the shorter forms like *fabula* or *exemplum* (fable, anecdote, etc.), and even the direct speech which they are prepared to admit is not necessarily dialogue, for they divide *sermocinatio* (roughly, "direct speech") into at least two and sometimes three varieties: dialogue and monologue, which may be subdivided again into a remark made aloud to another person and mental reflection or soliloquy.[6] In the works of San Pedro there is more than one example of the employment of *sermocinatio* in this fashion. So, for instance, in his *Sermón,* his brief recounting of the tale of Pyramus and

Thisbe ends with his reporting in direct speech the words of
Thisbe to her dead lover, just before she commits suicide.[7] It is
odd, but not, I think, significant, that the two examples in *Prison
of Love* should also be the words of female suicides: they occur
in the dying Leriano's defense of women, when he cites as
examples of virtuous women Lucretia (she who was raped by
Tarquin) and Doña Isabel de las Casas, who rejected medical
advice to take a husband after the death of Don Pedro Girón.
In each case, San Pedro reports in direct speech their precise
words.[8]

In following the recommendations of the theorists, whose
instructions are, of course, directed to writers in Latin, Diego
de San Pedro had quite clearly one overriding consideration in
mind: to create in Spanish a work which could not be said to
be inferior to works written in Latin. His adoption of a highly
rhetorical and heavily Latinized prose style was obviously
intended to serve the same purpose. It is the one trait which
may be said unequivocally to distinguish the "Renaissance"
writer: his notion that the ancients could be equalled, his
ambition to create in the vernacular a literature which might
rival or at least approximate to classical literature.[9] So far as
the style of *Arnalte and Lucenda* is concerned, San Pedro was
to realize later that he had erred; but in his aversion to "dialogue"
and his preference for the exchange of monologues, he made
no change when he came to write *Prison of Love*.

The justification for San Pedro's choosing to use this kind of
formal discourse can, however, be taken a step further. In
using the also rigidly dictated rules for epistolary composition
to guide the composition of his units of formal discourse, San
Pedro had very nearly stumbled upon the epistolary novel, with
all its attendant advantages and disadvantages.

III   *The Beginnings of the Epistolary Novel*

The history of the long, slow evolution of the epistolary novel
proper, that is, the novel narrated solely by means of the inter-
change of letters, is too complex to pursue in detail here.[10] It
is marked by a series of false starts, and is intimately related to
the development of that specialized art form, the letter, which
has a very much longer history as a literary form.

The epistle, however functional in intent, had from the time of the Greeks a set of rules to govern its composition. The form was even more assiduously cultivated by the Romans, and we find that busy magistrates and politicians not only composed their letters in the prescribed form (both by following the rules and imitating models), but took care to keep copies, to polish them when necessary, and to publish their correspondence; while in the Middle Ages the composition of letters became a literary discipline which formed an important part of the rhetorical curriculum of the schools.[11] Following the rules and suggestions of the treatises known as *artes dictaminis*, letter-writing manuals, letters were written as a purely literary exercise, and could therefore be directed to quite fictional addressees, or to famous historical or mythological personages.[12]

The rules of the *artes dictaminis* not only divided the epistle into its essential component parts, but offered suggestions about what might go into each. For instance, after the *salutatio* (still an essential constituent of all letters, even if it is reduced to the rudimentary formula of "Dear Sir"), there came the *exordium*, in which the letter-writer was supposed to give the recipient some indication of why he should bother to pay any attention to the letter at all. One suggestion of the theorists is that the writer might employ one of the formulae of the so-called *captatio benevolentiae*, the winning of good will. In a love letter, a few words praising the lady might suffice; otherwise any striking remark which might provoke interest or the curiosity to read further would serve; and some theorists even suggest that the mere promise to be brief might suffice to persuade the recipient to go on reading.[13] Amidst all the perhaps needless elaboration of these treatises, there is to be found, in fact, a good deal of thoughtful observation and sound common sense.

I shall not attempt here to set out, even in summary, the rules of medieval epistolary composition, but simply note that Diego de San Pedro was thoroughly acquainted with them and observed them scrupulously. Indeed, the letters which he composed for *Arnalte and Lucenda* were to become in their turn models for imitation, and one of the English translations of the novel was actually used as a manual of rhetoric, and the divisions of the epistle, and the devices used, were identified by annotations printed in the margin.[14]

To return to the epistolary novel: although there were sundry pieces of prose fiction which made some use of letters, there existed no work in prose which might be called an epistolary novel. On the other hand, something rather like a very small-scale epistolary narrative had developed in verse. The first well-known writer to transpose the epistle from prose to verse was Ovid, who in his *Heroides* or *Epistulae heroidum* (*Heroines' Letters*) composed metrical love letters for fourteen[15] legendary heroines, addressed to their absent lovers or husbands; and an important innovation, apparently suggested to him by his friend Sabinus,[16] was his grouping into pairs—letter and reply—of an additional six epistles probably added to the collection at a later date.

The same step, possibly under the influence of Ovid, was again taken at a much later date by the poets of northern France and of Italy, who, in imitating the Provençal *saluts d'amors*, verse love letters, hit upon the idea of elaborating an exchange of such letters. The most developed examples of these series are the Italian *contrasti*, which employ the sonnet form, and extend to an exchange of something between six and ten "letters," and, exceptionally, in the case of one series by Ciacco dell'Anguillaia, to thirty-two.[17] We are still, however, some distance away from an epistolary novel. It is largely a matter of scale, but it is one of those cases where a difference of quantity becomes a difference of quality. The *contrasti* are little more than a series of usually witty exchanges between a lover and his lady, and although the arguments and postures of the suitor may achieve a change in the lady's attitude by the end of the series, this purely internal plot can hardly be called a plot at all. No external events impinge upon the relationship; no elapse of time is implied or is necessary to the furtherance of the "story"; and, above all, the sonnets of the *contrasti* do not allow scope for that detailed examination of the emotions and reactions of the correspondents which is permitted by the more spacious and leisurely treatment offered by the epistolary or sentimental novel. (I shall return to the problem of the distinction of these two forms.)

IV *San Pedro's Success and Failure*

The credit for achieving the first epistolary novel—in any language—must go to Juan de Segura, whose *Proceso de cartas de amores* (*Exchange of Love Letters*) was first printed in 1548. But he could hardly have taken that decisive step without the prior work of Diego de San Pedro. In fact, it is fairly clear that San Pedro succeeded in creating what was almost the epistolary novel largely by accident, and that, with hindsight, he regretted that he had not taken the decisive and logical step.

Both *Arnalte and Lucenda* and *Prison of Love* are described by some modern critics as "epistolary novels," and while I feel that this is a mistake and that we should reserve the term for novels told wholly through letters, San Pedro did come closer to the true epistolary novel than any of his predecessors, and his near-success was due, I believe, to an evolutionary accident. In classical rhetoric the two principal divisions of prose composition were the letter and the discourse; but the discourse, *oratio*, was that persuasive political speech or that legal argument which is exemplified in the orations of someone like Demosthenes or Cicero. In the Middle Ages, on the other hand, the two principal divisions of prose composition were the letter and the sermon. The letter followed the old classical rules (with some medieval elaborations), and the sermon, with even more elaborations, adopted much of what the classical theorists had written about persuasive discourse. The short speech, such as that which might be appropriate for a declaration of love, had no rules of its own, and Diego de San Pedro employed for it the structure which had been devised for the epistle. If he had only arranged matters so that all Arnalte's speeches were prefaced by a different form of words ("and what I wrote to her was this," instead of "and what I said to her was this"), he would have been even closer to creating the epistolary novel.

In fact, there is some reason for supposing that Diego de San Pedro did consider and discard the idea of telling his story entirely by means of letters, for in the preface to *Arnalte and Lucenda* he makes the following cryptic statement: "Actually, I had thought of presenting my story in a different fashion, but, although it would have been more subtle, it might have been less pleasing, and so I abandoned the idea" (*Bien pensé por otro estilo mis razones seguir, pero aunque fuera más sotil fuera menos agradable, y desta causa la obra del pensamiento dexé*).[18] Taken by itself, of course, this could mean almost anything, but there is a very curious line in the opening stanzas of his *Contempt of Fortune* in which he reviews (and condemns as frivolous) some of his earlier work. His *Sermon* and his *Prison of Love* are identified by name, but he then mentions "that series of paired love letters" (*aquellas cartas de amores / escriptas de dos en dos*) and does not refer in any other way to *Arnalte and Lucenda*. He seems to be claiming that *Arnalte and Lucenda* *was* an epistolary novel. (It is evident that his self-condemnation has a certain ambivalence about it.) It is as though with the gift of hindsight Diego de San Pedro regretted his failure to follow up his idea of presenting his story in a more subtle way, and at the same time wished to claim that he had had the idea and that, however imperfectly the result matched his initial conception, he had in some way actually created the epistolary novel by compiling an exchange of love letters.

V *Comic Elements in* Arnalte and Lucenda

Before looking at the way in which the epistolary novel (a primarily formal genre) is related to the sentimental novel (a primarily conceptual genre), there are some aspects of the story of Arnalte which need closer examination. Regula Langbehn-Rohland was the first to draw attention in print to what she regarded as some rather disturbing comic elements in *Arnalte and Lucenda,* such as Arnalte's dressing as a woman in order to stand next to Lucenda in church, or his sending his page to inspect the rubbish thrown out of Lucenda's house in order to determine the fate of his letter.[19] And the list can be readily extended. I have found that students have considered laughable or absurd Arnalte's going on a hunting holiday to recover from the devastation wrought by unrequited love, Arnalte's offering himself to Lucenda as a substitute for the husband he has slain, Arnalte's arguing that he has done Lucenda a great favor in killing Elierso in as much as he has provided her with the opportunity to demonstrate her virtue in forgiving him, Arnalte's attempting to justify his recitation of *The Seven Sorrows of Our Lady* by saying that it would help him to forget his own sorrows, and so on.

The difficulty which we at once run into is in knowing whether San Pedro intended us to take all this seriously, whether his contemporary readers would have taken it seriously, and whether we are justified in regarding some of these things as comically incongruous. And the problem is complicated by the fact that some of the motifs have a perfectly respectable literary ancestry, and first occur in contexts which are not at all comic. The trip to the country, or even more specifically the hunting holiday, was a standard prescription for sundry maladies, and was even suggested by serious medical authorities as the treatment indicated in cases of love.[20] The motif of a man's supplanting the man he has killed goes back a very long way (at least as far as the myth of Oedipus), but it occurs in a context exactly parallel to San Pedro's in Chrétien de Troyes's *Yvain*, where Yvain marries Laudine after killing her husband, while in the *Mocedades de Rodrigo* the Cid marries Jimena after he has killed her father. Even Arnalte's dressing as a woman to get close to Lucenda may have as its source (does have, according to Schevill)[21] the story of Achilles and Deidamia as related by Ovid in his *Ars amatoria* (1, 697 ff.).

While the citation of literary antecedents may not be entirely convincing, we have some evidence of contemporary reaction which might lead us to doubt whether Diego de San Pedro intended to be funny, for both the French and Italian translators of *Arnalte and Lucenda* added comments of their own to express their severe condemnation of Lucenda's wanton cruelty and their admiration for the nobility and heroism of Arnalte.[22] But in spite of all this, I do not believe that we are guilty of unjustifiable anachronism if we insist upon perceiving incongruities and gross lapses of taste in *Arnalte and Lucenda*. There is, moreover, some reason to suppose that they are deliberate.

Dr. Langbehn-Rohland (*loc. cit.*) has identified, as the factor which produces these comic elements, the incongruity, the absurd contrast, between Arnalte's conduct and the high-flown idealism which he expresses in his speeches and letters, and also between

Diego de San Pedro's elevated style and the mundane details
which he sometimes employs it to record. What is absurd in
the novel surely does stem from such dissonances. But while
this is undoubtedly true, the problem presented here by *Arnalte*
is by no means unique in medieval or even Golden Age literature. It presents itself in even more extreme form in Aeneas
Sylvius Piccolomini's *Historia de duobus amantibus* (*Story of
Two Lovers*),[23] written in 1444, where the noble hero Euryalus
seduces and abandons Lucretia, a married woman, and she dies
of grief. The novel closes with the extraordinary statement that
Euryalus was very sad until the Emperor found for him, from
among the noble families of the Dukes of Germany, a virgin,
rich, prudent, and very beautiful, to be his wife. And it is this
same heroic Euryalus, represented as a gallant and handsome
captain of noble birth, who is also shown to us hiding at the
unexpected return of Lucretia's husband, quaking with fear,
and vowing to God that if only he escapes alive he will never
more succumb to love, or permit a woman's tongue to seduce
him. This is both comic and grotesque.

The same sort of problem arises also, as Barry Ife has shown, in
sundry Golden Age retellings of the tale of Pyramus and Thisbe,
not just by Góngora—and Góngora's apparent ambivalence has
left many critics uneasy if not baffled—but by a series of poets.[24]
And the grossest incongruity of all derives directly from the
earliest extant version of the story presented by Ovid in his
Metamorphoses, and that is the mock-heroic comparison of
Pyramus spurting blood with a ruptured water pipe in a city
street.[25]

There is, however, one constant common element in all these
problems: somewhere in the background we invariably find
Ovid. The trick of taking some tragic story—a suicide, a drowning, a human sacrifice[26]—and wrecking the solemnity of the
moment by introducing a bathetic comparison or making some
comically incongruous observation is a feature of Ovid's writing
which has not yet been thoroughly investigated. Classical scholars seem to have the habit of referring to the use of this device
as "the grotesque" in Ovid, a term which does not indicate suffi-
ciently exactly its deflationary nature. Nor does it originate with
Ovid, for the Greek Alexandrian poets had a taste for this kind

of thing. Callimachus and his pupil, and later literary enemy, Apollonius of Rhodes, quarreled in one episode of a bitter literary controversy between the writers of relatively short poems (the *epyllia*) and the composers of long, traditional epic. But both, in true Alexandrian fashion, consistently underplay the heroic deeds of mythology and are given to slipping in what the critics term "humorous remarks." Jason, the protagonist of Apollonius's *Argonautica*, has even been called an anti-hero.[27]

Now it is well known that the Middle Ages took Ovid's jokes seriously. They wholly failed to perceive the tongue-in-cheek element in his *Ars amatoria*, and it is indeed recorded that it was read allegorically as an edifying text by nuns;[28] while the story of Pyramus and Thisbe was generally taken as a moral tale, a warning against jumping too hastily to conclusions.[29] But when we are dealing with Pope Pius II (that is, Aeneas Sylvius Piccolomini), we should be very rash to think in teams of medieval naïveté. Aeneas Sylvius knew his Ovid, and he was a highly sophisticated scholar; so that while his *Historia de duobus amantibus* is filled with motifs and verbal reminiscenses borrowed from Ovid,[30] there is hardly any doubt that the portrayal of Euryalus's cowardice is meant to be comic, that the conclusion is calculatedly cynical, and even that, when Aeneas Sylvius borrowed for Euryalus, from the pseudo-Ovidian *Pulex*, the expression of a desire to be a flea to creep around Lucretia's body, he was aware of the comic bathos and incongruity of the conceit.[31]

The case of Diego de San Pedro is less unequivocal. And there is, perhaps, no way of demonstrating conclusively that he was fully conscious of what he was doing when he inserted the episodes, motifs, and remarks which can strike modern readers as incongruous or comic. But it is perhaps significant not only that his "burlesque" *Sermon* matches Ovid's *Ars amatoria* very well in tone—there is a distinct tongue-in-cheek element about it—but that he should have chosen for the *exemplum*, the elevating anecdote which rounds it off, precisely the tale of Pyramus and Thisbe.[32] Perhaps we should be prepared to bear in mind the possibility that Diego de San Pedro is more Ovidian than he has so far been perceived to be.

VI *The Sentimental Novel and the Ovidian Tale*

Menéndez Pelayo was the first to identify and label as a distinct genre in Spanish literature the "sentimental novel" (*la novela sentimental*)[33] and now almost all historians of literature habitually use the term, as do the critics who have written about one or another of these so-called sentimental novels.[34] Some scholars have reopened the question of whether such a genre can be said to exist at all, but they have invariably concluded, with whatever misgivings and qualifications, that it does,[35] even though Armando Durán, attempting a structuralist comparison of the sentimental novel and the romance of chivalry, felt himself obliged to separate the sentimental novel into two distinct varieties, the "sentimental novel proper" (*la novela propiamente sentimental*) and the "erotic novel" (*la novela erótica*).[36]

While the two novels of Diego de San Pedro are quite invariably accepted as part of the canon, there are probably few critics who would agree in subsuming under the label of "sentimental novel" all the works which have at different times been so designated. They are: Juan Rodríguez del Padrón's *Siervo libre de amor* (*Free Slave of Love*), written around 1450, the Constable of Portugal's *Sátira de felice e infelice vida* (*Happy and Unhappy Life*),[37] of the same period, the anonymous *Triste deleitación* (*Sad Delight* or perhaps *Delightful Sadness*), which is also early, the two novels of Juan de Flores, *Grisel and Mirabella* and *Grimalte and Gradissa,* both first published about 1495, the continuation of *Prison of Love* composed by Nicolás Núñez (1496), Pedro Manuel de Urrea's *Penitencia de amor* (*Penance of Love*), written in 1499 but not printed until 1514, the anonymous *Cuestión de amor* (*Debate about Love*), printed in 1513, Ludovico or Luis Escrivá's *Veneris tribunal* (*Lawcourt of Love*), which appeared in 1537, and Juan de Segura's *Proceso de cartas de amores,* the very first epistolary novel, which was printed in 1548.[38]

Critics have pointed to a series of features which a number of these stories have in common: references to mythology and classical allusions, Latinizing syntax, allegory, visions and dreams, mixture of verse and prose, letters, autobiographical form, didactic elements, etc., and occasionally a critic has seized on one particular feature as *the* characteristic which distinguishes the "sentimental novel" from other varieties of contemporary fiction. For Millares Carlo it is the autobiographical element (he would have been on only slightly surer ground if he had termed it first-person narrative).[39] For Cvitanovic it is the didactic element.[40] But although some of these features do tend to recur, not one of them appears consistently in all or even most of the works which have been categorized as "sentimental novels." At the very best they form a singularly heterogeneous genre. Even to divide them into two kinds, as Durán does, helps us very little, for in his classification Aeneas Sylvius's *Historia de duobus amantibus* is placed in the same category as *Prison of Love*, in contradistinction to *Arnalte and Lucenda*, while the works of Rodríguez del Padrón and Juan de Segura, which contain tales within tales, have each one story classified as an "erotic novel" and one as a "sentimental novel." A change of designation to, for instance, "courtly romance," which could be argued to be more appropriate for San Pedro, does not solve the problem of whether a genre exists.

To define the sentimental novel at all, one must resort to cruder criteria than have generally been applied, and distinguish a little more clearly between form and content. The only consistent formal criterion which distinguishes the sentimental novel is that it is short—short, that is, in comparison with other varieties of the fiction of its time, and, in particular, enormously shorter than any of the romances of chivalry. As for the content, the sentimental (or erotic) novel is invariably a love story, and, much more than the romance of chivalry, it tends to concentrate its attention on emotional states and internal conflicts rather than on external action. At the very least, its focus of interest is the love affair itself, and amorous intrigue displaces combat and adventure as the principal ingredient of the plot. It is, quite simply, a short love story.

If we could accept that "sentimental novel" is merely a synonym for "short love story," we should have no further difficulties to face. But the short love story is self-evidently not a "genre," and it is clearly not what critics mean when they speak of the "sentimental novel" as a "genre"; if it is to serve any useful purpose at all, the term must imply an aesthetic convention

which shapes the character of the works written in that convention, and this is the point at which the notion of genre begins
to falsify the picture of Spanish literary history. It is by no
means demonstrated that either Diego de San Pedro or Juan de
Flores knew or was influenced by any of the "sentimental
novels" written by their Peninsular precursors: *Siervo libre,
Sátira de felice e infelice vida, Triste deleitación*.[41] And if one
extends the category to include such obviously influential works
as Boccaccio's *Fiammetta*, Aeneas Sylvius's *Historia de duobus
amantibus*, and some of the quite long versified love stories
which one finds in fourteenth- and fifteenth-century French literature, the boundaries become vague indeed.[42] It is not much
more helpful to treat the earlier storytellers as "precursors" and
date the origins of the sentimental novel proper from the works
of San Pedro and Juan de Flores, for there are substantial differences between these two,[43] and while the influence of both
was in various directions very great indeed, there were not
many direct imitations of their works, and the late "sentimental
novels" owe rather more to new Italian influences than to
Spanish antecedents.

Schevill argued that the works which Menéndez Pelayo had
called "sentimental novels" would be more appropriately termed
Ovidian stories or Ovidian novels, in as much as they all contain quotations, precepts, motifs, and themes borrowed from
the erotic works of Ovid.[44] But one then discovers that Schevill
is obliged to exclude from his new category of "Ovidian tale"
both Juan Rodríguez's *Free Slave of Love* and San Pedro's
Prison of Love, and that he fails to mention at all other works
which later critics have chosen to classify as sentimental novels.
Schevill's suggestion has not been picked up—perhaps because
of the obvious objections to his proposal—by the historians of
Spanish literature. But he was by no means wholly mistaken.

Arnalte and Lucenda, like Boccaccio's *Fiammetta* and Pius
II's *Historia de duobus amantibus*, is fabricated from Ovidian
material. Schevill has pointed out some of the numerous direct
reminiscences of and quotations from Ovid: precepts like *el
secreto es del amador corona* ("secrecy is the finest virtue of
the perfect lover"), maxims like *todas las cosas que haver no
se pueden son estimadas, y después de havidas suelen en meno-*

sprecio venir ("after you get what you want you don't want it"), as well as sundry motifs and situations: the use of messengers and letters, Arnalte's falling in love with Lucenda at her father's funeral, Arnalte's disguising himself as a woman, his confiding his secret, with disastrous results, to a friend, Lucenda's yielding to the threat of his absence, and so on. And there is yet more, in particular in the attitude of the author to love, which might well be termed Ovidian. But even more significant is the fact that Schevill was unable to find in *Prison of Love*, apart from the use of letters, anything whatsoever which he could attribute to the influence or example of Ovid.

There is really not the slightest doubt that both *Arnalte and Lucenda* and Aeneas Sylvius's *Historia de duobus amantibus* are "Ovidian tales," whether or not they are also "sentimental novels," and *Prison of Love* is, equally without question, *not* Ovidian. The attempt to impose categories on the resistant mass of medieval literature has resulted in some confusion, and quite certainly in a distortion of the history of the evolution of the "sentimental novel." Clearly, a number of very diverse currents come together at the end of the fifteenth century. Boccaccio's *Fiammetta* is Ovidian, the extended and passionate complaint of a woman abandoned by her lover. Pius II's *Euryalus et Lucretia* is Ovidian, but is steeped in the atmosphere of Boccaccio's *Decameron*, not his *Fiammetta*: cynical, sometimes funny, often obscene. But other short love stories such as *Free Slave of Love* emerge from a different tradition: ultimately from the later French elaboration of Arthurian romance, the shorter verse-romances in which there is a shift of emphasis from chivalry to love. Other ideas about love, set out in verse or in prose treatises, also contributed to the formation of the "sentimental novel" of the late fifteenth century.

It is, on the whole, useful to group in some way the short love stories of the later Middle Ages, but the heterogeneity of the tales within this group is such that the term "genre" is probably misapplied in this context, since there are so very few generalizations one can safely make about them. And if *Prison of Love* is the perfect archetype of the sentimental novel or courtly romance, it is important to comprehend how it came to be created, and to appreciate the fundamental shift in San

Pedro's ideas which made it possible. *Prison of Love* is an Ovidian tale shorn of Ovidianism, and a crucial step in its genesis was San Pedro's having to write his *Sermon* on love.

VII   *Arnalte's Imperfections*

As I have noted, one factor which perhaps contributes to the incongruous comic effect of certain passages of *Arnalte and Lucenda* is the contrast between Arnalte's high-flown protestations and his actual conduct. What we find in *Arnalte and Lucenda* is an attitude on the part of the author which might be described as semi-Ovidian. If San Pedro does not treat it all as a joke, at the same time he does not seem to take it quite as seriously as he does later. Arnalte repeatedly insists on his wholehearted and sincere devotion to Lucenda and on his readiness to "serve" her; but simultaneously he demands a series of favors from her, argues that she is in some way indebted to him for his being in love with her, and blames her for his sufferings. If Arnalte is much less of an egotistic trifler than Euryalus, he is still very far from being the perfect lover whom San Pedro portrayed in the hero of his *Prison of Love*.

Part of the resemblance between Arnalte and Euryalus stems from the fact that each embarks on a systematic campaign to make a conquest of the lady of whom he has become enamored, and employs sundry stratagems of the kind recommended by Ovid in his *Ars amatoria,* that "amatory art" or "manual of love" whose title might be more accurately translated as *How to Win and Keep a Woman.*

It has frequently been observed that Ovid's *Ars amatoria* is not really about love at all, but about the techniques of seduction. This, however, is less than just. It is only Book I which provides hints and tips on how to capture the affections of a woman; Book II goes on to the question of how, having won her love, the lover may retain it; and Book III offers advice to the woman. It is abundantly clear that Ovid is concerned with genuine affection and the duration of a love affair (*ut longe tempore duret amor,* I, 38), not with an ephemeral and merely sexual conquest. Throughout the *Ars amatoria,* and despite a certain characteristically Ovidian ambivalence, Ovid demonstrates a sensitivity, sympathy, and even tenderness which belie the superficial cynicism of many of his odd remarks.

The *Ars amatoria* is a difficult work to pin down. The traditional interpretation is that it is basically a nonserious book, which makes fun simultaneously of a whole tradition of how-to-do-it manuals, of the idea that "love" can also be reduced to a set of rules and techniques, and even of any solemnity about "love" at all. But if one were obliged to formulate some sensible, concrete advice about the best places to find a girl in order to strike up an acquaintanceship, about how to make the initial approach, about how to provoke her interest and make oneself agreeable to her, and so forth, one would be reduced to duplicating, with perfectly serious intent, a great deal of Ovid's advice (*mutatis mutandis*). What might then be adjudged "cynical" is only the far from unrealistic proposition that it is possible to manipulate the emotions and attitudes of others not by sincerity or natural charm, but by learning and obeying certain rules. And even then, as Ovid says, the emotions which we begin by feigning we may end by experiencing quite genuinely.[45]

It is doubtful that Ovid would have found much to censure in the attitude or conduct of Arnalte apart from his resort to violence or his final decision to languish despairingly in the wilderness. That Arnalte, having fallen in love with Lucenda, should resort to all the tricks and stratagems he can think of in order to approach her and win her affections, would have seemed to Ovid perfectly natural and right. But Arnalte behaves in ways which San Pedro forbids in his *Sermon* and which simply do not occur to Leriano. He sends a letter by a page who, at his master's instructions, forces it upon Lucenda; he disguises himself as a woman and thrusts his unwanted attentions upon her in church, at mass, on Christmas Eve; he has musicians serenade her from the street; he insinuates his page into her household; he wears at a tournament a device which proclaims his passion; he forces her by his importunity in public to dance with him; he pushes another letter into her pocket while she is standing by the Queen and cannot protest; he follows her to her room; he has his page hunt through the waste paper thrown out of her house; he tries to keep clandestine watch on her from the neighboring house of his friend Elierso; he lies to her and pretends that he is going to leave the court; he uses his sister, Lucenda's closest friend, to press his suit; and, of course, he ends by killing her husband.

Arnalte stands condemned by the standards of Leriano or San Pedro's *Sermon;* and his fault is basically his self-interest. The ideal lover, as San Pedro is later to insist, "wants what *she* wants" (*quiere lo que ella quiere*); the ideal lover gives his loved one's interests the highest priority, regardless of his own desires or welfare; the ideal lover is happy to suffer all the anguish of unrequited love without complaint; the ideal lover humbly adores his mistress and does not venture to molest, to embarrass, to importune, or to criticize her.

But if to modern readers Arnalte's behavior seems not quite to match the conduct expected of a gentleman, Diego de San Pedro must not be accused of any lack of sensibility. It is quite obvious, from the continuation of *Prison of Love* written by Nicolás Núñez and from the comments of the foreign translators of *Arnalte and Lucenda,* that many if not most of San Pedro's male contemporaries found nothing wrong in Arnalte's conduct and a great deal wrong with Lucenda's. They thought that she had been both cruel and ungrateful. As Melibea says in *Celestina* (XIV), justifying her own surrender to Calisto, "love is satisfied with no repayment but love" (*el amor no admite sino solo amor por paga*), and this notion is implicit throughout Arnalte's speeches and letters, and is quite often explicit: Lucenda is in his debt. Even in his very first letter to her he makes the point half a dozen times: "I thoroughly deserve your favors" (*tus mercedes ... mucho merescidas te las tengo*), "see how much you are in my debt" (*mira en cuánto cargo me eres*), "so that you shall be even more obliged to me" (*porque más obligada me seas*), "I am confident that you will not be ungrateful" (*mayor confiança ... en tu conoscimiento tengo*), "it is impossible that reward should not be given where it is seen to be deserved" (*no puede ser que donde se meresce el galardón no se dé*).[46]

But in pressing his suit in this fashion—accusing Lucenda of cruelty and ingratitude, demanding that she show him favor, proclaiming her in his debt—Arnalte seemingly perceives no

discrepancy between his demands and criticisms and his protestations of undying devotion to her and readiness to "serve"
her in any way she desires. The incongruity reaches its highest
point when, having killed her husband (without of course,
taking her wishes into account), he argues that she is now even
further in his debt, since he has provided her with the opportunity to make manifest one of her hidden virtues by forgiving
him. Lucenda—understandably, we may feel—does not even
deign to answer and retires to a convent. Arnalte, though
undoubtedly in love, has no "proper" conception of what love
means or how he should behave: it is for him an unmerited
catastrophe which has fallen upon him; he did not want to
fall in love and made strenuous attempts to resist, but found
it beyond his power; it brings him only misery and grief; and
he is wholly obsessed with securing, by whatever means, the
"remedy" for his pain.

Diego de San Pedro has, in a sense, fallen between two
stools; or, giving him more credit, he has reached in *Arnalte*
the halfway house between the *Story of Two Lovers* and *Prison
of Love*. Arnalte has recourse to Ovidian stratagems when he
is suffering from a malady far more intense, powerful, and
genuinely dangerous (to health and life) than the emotion
known to Ovid. Ovid's lover is to set out to look for a suitable
girl; San Pedro's lover is struck down, an unwilling victim,
when he least expects it. Something, somewhere, does not quite
fit in *Arnalte and Lucenda*. It is as though San Pedro on the
one hand accepted the medieval view of love as an overwhelm-
ing, painful, obsessive, paradoxical, death-dealing passion, such
as it is represented in the love poetry of the period, but on the
other hand had private reservations, for the concept of a grand
passion is subtly undermined—perhaps deliberately, perhaps
unconsciously. It was certainly a mistake to insert the poem
about Isabella, for the object of Arnalte's hyperbolically-
expressed passion is rather conspicuously not remotely in the
same class; the poem on the Sorrows of the Virgin was also a
mistake, perhaps not so much because of a damaging effect
on the heroine, but because Arnalte's "sorrows" are exposed
by the comparison as too trivial to make such a fuss over;
Arnalte's black palace and nightly self-flagellation are made

faintly ridiculous, when the noise made by the moaning household prevents the Author from getting some sleep; some of the arguments which Arnalte uses in his speeches and letters are so specious as to be absurd; the eruption of violence at the climax of the tale smacks of melodrama rather than tragedy; and, above all, Arnalte's importunate insistence on his own worth tends to underline the unworthiness of his behavior, the Ovidian shamelessness of his conduct, and his unheroic inadequacy as a lover.

VIII *The Style of* Arnalte and Lucenda

As I have explained, the units of composition of *Arnalte and Lucenda* are set rhetorical pieces. Even the passages of narrative which link the speeches and letters are of a length comparable with the other set pieces, for *narratio* was itself classed as a type of digression within a discourse.[47] That the very structure of the whole work is completely "rhetorical" does not seem to have occurred to the numerous critics who have complained that San Pedro's style is "too rhetorical." Whatever antecedents or models San Pedro had to guide him, there is a sense in which we can say that, at least in Castilian, he created a new art form, and created it by following as closely as possible the precepts of medieval rhetoricians who intended their instructions to apply to writing in Latin. The style he employed in *Arnalte and Lucenda* may have its faults, but they are the faults of an extremist who, not for the only time, went a little too far. But it is possible to say rather specifically just what those faults are. It is absurd to use "rhetorical" as a dismissive term, just as it is hopelessly inadequate to employ such vague words as "antithetical" or "parallelistic" to describe the style. To understand properly San Pedro's goal and his achievement, we must employ the appropriate rhetorical terminology.

Before we look at the specific devices which San Pedro uses, there are some general points to be made about his language. San Pedro was obviously aiming at writing in the most elevated and artistic style he could contrive—and I use "elevated" in a strictly technical sense: rhetorical theory allowed for levels of style appropriate to the level of dignity of the subject matter.

And one general way in which he attempted to "raise" his language was by Latinizing it, above all in its syntax. While Diego de San Pedro is not a grossly neologizing writer so far as his vocabulary is concerned, he follows some earlier writers in making exaggerated and unwarranted changes in the syntax of Castilian prose by, for instance, obeying Latin rules for the employment of the subjunctive, and, very conspicuously, by postponing the verb. The Spanish verb is unnaturally placed in final position in something like 75 percent of subordinate clauses and some 50 percent of main clauses in *Arnalte and Lucenda*. Consider, for example, the following passage, in which I have italicized the verbs:[48] "Otras cosas muchas comigo mesmo *fablé*, las cuales, por enojoso no *ser*, en el callar *dexo*. Y después que ya de mi despedido *fui*, con mis pensamientos el navío de mis passiones a remar *comencé*; pero como la tormenta de las ansias grande *fuese*, nunca puerto de descanso *fallé*; y como en el grave cuidado los debidos passatiempos *olvidase*, muy poco el palacio *seguía*, ni al rey de ver *curava*; y como él a mis amigos mucho por mi *preguntase*, de ir una noche a palacio *acordé*." The passage is not untranslatable, but the word order cannot be copied in English without producing grotesque effects: "with my thoughts the boat of my sufferings to row I began," "very little the palace I frequented, nor the King to see I bothered," etc. The effect, though obtrusive, is perhaps a shade less unacceptable in Spanish than in English; and one not merely accidental by-product of the postponement of the verb is the frequent achievement of a rhyme.

The rhyme which repeatedly occurs is certainly deliberate; this is obvious because of the insistent frequency of such matched pairs of clauses as *e si no te valiere, a la razón requiere,* or *las bozes della su dormir de Lucenda recordar pudieron; pero los gritos de mis angustias nunca su galardón vieron,* because it can be accounted for in terms of the accepted "colors of rhetoric," and because San Pedro's passages of rhyming prose exactly match the Latin rhyme-prose which is to be found in such works as Thomas à Kempis's *Imitatio Christi.*[49]

The rhyming effects are particularly noticeable, as are also several other rhetorical devices (again members of that class of ornament called *colores rhetorici*), which have been labeled by certain modern writers as "figures of sound" or "acoustic conceits." They include a kind of alliteration known as *paromoion* or *paranomeon*, and a trick of reduplicating word roots (which constitutes two distinct figures in Latin, *annominatio* and *traductio*, scarcely separable in Spanish), such as "tan *aquexado* con tu *quexar*, que es *forçado* que me *fuerce* para lo que mis *señales señalan claramente declararte.*" In addition, the author strives for rhythmic effects, which can be at times so marked and so sustained that it is possible to set his prose out as verse, most often in octosyllabic lines.

All these sound effects, the rhyme, the rhythm, the alliteration, the jingle of reduplication, are devices which San Pedro was later to abandon, as we shall see. But the acoustic effects constitute only one aspect, admittedly obtrusive and perhaps offensive, of San Pedro's use of rhetoric in *Arnalte and Lucenda*, and basically, in the use of other devices in the category of "easy ornament" (*ornamentum facile*, the so-called "colors"), in the use of "difficult ornament" (*ornamentum difficile*, tropes or figures of thought), and in having recourse to the techniques of *amplificatio*, the much-praised style of *Prison of Love* is no different from the style of *Arnalte and Lucenda*. I shall leave therefore, for the chapter on *Prison of Love*, an examination of the constants in San Pedro's art-prose.

There is one final point to make here: as the theorists explained, style was to be matched to content. For "high" matters a writer must employ a suitably "high" style, and for "low" matters much plainer and less ornamented language. In making the style of *Arnalte and Lucenda* so consistently high-flown, San Pedro offended, not just against the tenets of the new rhetoric which came in with humanism, but against the precepts even of medieval rhetoric. To describe mundane activities in elevated language tends to produce something of a comic effect; to use elaborate high-sounding rhetorical prose to describe a page's scrabbling ignominiously among discarded waste paper to find out if the lady has torn up his master's letter begins to verge on the ludicrous. But did it not lend itself to travesty? Whether Diego de San Pedro was himself conscious of this effect—which is not wholly impossible—is something of which we may never be quite sure. To ascribe this discrepancy between style and matter to sheer obtuseness and insensitivity raises the difficulty of explaining San Pedro's intelligence and sensitivity in other works and in other areas; and it is perhaps just credible that it is a trick which parallels Ovid's inflated mythological digressions in the *Ars amatoria* or his use of solemn philosophical maxims to justify the most trivial and even cynical piece of practical advice. The problem is far from being solved.

CHAPTER 6

Sermón (Sermon)

I *A Code of Behavior for Lovers*

AT some date in the 1480's after the composition and circula-
tion of *Arnalte and Lucenda,* some ladies of the court
demanded that Diego de San Pedro should write a sermon, "for
they desired to hear him preach."[1] They would surely have been
grievously disappointed if San Pedro had chosen to hold forth
in the vein of his *Versified Passion,* but our author was in no
doubt about what was required of him. As he explains in the
preamble to his *Sermon,* the writer or speaker adjusts his matter
to his audience: with knights one talks of deeds of chivalry;
with the devout, of the Passion of Christ; with scholars, of the
pleasures of scholarship; and since he is now to preach to the
ladies, he will speak of the passion of love. (And note this
most characteristic trait of our author: the topic does not
determine the audience to whom the material will be addressed;
the audience determines the topic.)

It is, in fact, to a mixed audience that the sermon is directed,
and of its three sections, the first two consist of rules for the
men, and the third of advice to the ladies (an arrangement which
parallels that of the three books of Ovid's *Ars amatoria*). San
Pedro takes as his text an ingeniously concocted verse from a
fictitious Gospel according to St. Infatuation: *In patientia vestra
sustinete dolores vestros* ("Bear your sorrows in patience"),[2]
and each section of the sermon leads up to a repetition of the
text, translated into Spanish.

In the fashion habitual in the learned sermon, San Pedro
announces after giving his text how the sermon is to be divided
and of what he will treat in each part. The first part, he says
will show how ladies should be attended by their lovers (although the Spanish carries shadings not easy to translate: he
88

is to give an *ordenança*, a set of rules, laws, or commandments, to show how *amigas*, beloved ladies or mistresses, *se deven seguir*, should be followed, attended, obeyed or served). And the rules follow, with explanatory justification, and with sundry corollary subclauses.

The fundamental rule, from which all others flow, is that the lover must observe the most absolute secrecy, in order to avoid any breath of scandal which might touch upon his mistress's honor. He should die sooner than make his passion public. But he must also take the greatest possible care not to betray his ardor involuntarily: he must watch his words and his conduct; he must avoid using unreliable messengers, writing any compromising letters, or wearing embroidered devices which proclaim he is in love. He must be most especially careful if he has a rival, for this can lead to suspicion, despair, and indiscretion; to avoid self-betrayal through changes of color, trembling voice, angry looks, gnashing of teeth, and so on, he must exercise reason and patience until the fit of jealousy passes.

He must not haunt the street outside his beloved's house; he must let his face give nothing away; he must not indulge himself by wearing her colors or using the initial of her name in some device; he must never allow his gaze to linger on her.

However great the pain and anguish he is suffering, he must never be tempted to speak to others of his passion; and if he should find himself in very severe straits, then he should retire to some solitary place to think over his situation. While one thought may lead him to despair, another may bring him hope, but in any event he himself and his own thoughts are the only consolation he can permit himself, and, however hopeless his situation, he must "bear his sorrows in patience."

In the second part of the sermon, San Pedro offers some thoughts which may help to console the afflicted lover. The most important consideration is that he is suffering in a good cause. He should think of the excellence of the lady who has caused his passion; if he is unhappy it is because that is her wish, and he should be glad to suffer for her sake. However unkind she may be, he should have hope in his own constancy, for she may eventually yield; but he has no right to wish for anything but what his mistress wants. If she wants him to suffer, he must suffer; if she should want him to die, he must die; and if she should wish him to be damned, he must, body and soul, go obediently to Hell.

If his sufferings do bring him to the point of death, he has reason to be happy, for he could meet no more noble and honorable end, dying for love, constancy, loyalty, and reason. He can ask for nothing more from his beloved than the opportunity to prove his fortitude, bearing suffering in life, and meeting death obedient and unafraid. He must "bear his sorrows in patience."

Then, in the third part, San Pedro turns to the ladies, to suggest how they should treat a lover. They must do what they can to relieve his suffering, for, if they do not, they commit four different mortal sins: by abusing their power they fall into the sin of pride; by taking possession of the heart, life, and freedom of a man, and giving nothing in return, they are guilty of avarice; if they become annoyed by their lover's importunities, they fall into the sin of anger; and if they will not stir themselves to utter even a kind word, they show that they are slothful.

It is in the nature of lions and serpents to deal out death; but for a woman it is wholly unnatural. A woman's role is one of loving, succoring, and consoling. The worst fault of all is ingratitude, and to see their lovers languishing in an ecstasy of adoration, oblivious of what goes on around them, to see them despairing, ill, and weeping, and then do nothing to afford them relief is to show ingratitude and cruelty. The ladies may ask: How can we relieve their pain without putting our honor at risk? But all that is necessary is a kind word and a kind look. Their lovers will not and must not ask for other favors.

And as an exemplary story of compassion and love, San Pedro retells the tale of Pyramus and Thisbe, enjoining the ladies to be as compassionate as Thisbe. But if they insist on scorning their lovers, then the lovers must "bear their sorrows in patience." And he concludes with a little Latin prayer.

Diego de San Pedro's *Sermon* is basically and essentially an *ars amatoria,* a guide to lovers on how to behave. There are dozens of such manuals and treatises in the Middle Ages, both in Latin and the vernacular languages, and they are for the most part, like San Pedro's *Sermon, artes de honeste amandi,* that is, instructions on how the ideal lover should behave, and not hints and tips on how to make an amorous conquest.

San Pedro, however, has not chosen to write with unequivocal seriousness a treatise on the subject, but a sermon, which has been variously described as a burlesque sermon, a parody of a sermon, and a funny sermon. It is certainly not as simple as that, but we do have the difficult problem of knowing just how much in this "burlesque" sermon was said with perfectly serious intent.

II   *The Technique of the Sermon*

As usual, Diego de San Pedro demonstrates in his *Sermon* a complete mastery of the technique of the form. The medieval sermon was subject to ever more rigid and complex rules, and consisted of a number of distinct parts: the *thema,* the *prothema,* the invocation, the body of the sermon (usually divided into three parts), and a final *peroratio* or *clausio,* which included a prayer at the very end.[3] San Pedro appears to have had not the slightest difficulty in adapting himself to this form in all its complexity.

The *thema* in the genuine sermon had to be a quotation in Latin from the Scriptures (with due citation of the source). San Pedro, as we have seen, was obliged to manufacture his own text, but did so with an ingenious confection of genuine biblical phrases. It not only sounds authentic, but is in fact impeccable Christian teaching—even if it is to be subverted to irreligious ends. The *prothema* which followed was a translation and brief explanation of the *thema,* and the *invocatio* a brief prayer to ask for God's help in preaching the sermon. San Pedro quite simply addresses his invocation to Amor, the god of love.

In the body of the sermon, duly divided into the convenient number of parts, the preacher was to develop the explanation of his text, beginning with a brief statement of how he planned to approach it, and concluding with a brief summary of what his exposition had demonstrated. This conclusion, the *peroratio,* was also to include a final brief prayer. San Pedro uses the Christian-sounding prayer, *Ad quam gloriam nos perducat* ("And may he lead us into glory"), but the god whom he is addressing

is, of course, Amor, and *gloria* has in many texts of the period
unequivocal sexual connotations.[4]

III   *A Burlesque Sermon?*

The simple fact that San Pedro chooses the sermon form to
put across his ideas does not necessarily imply either that he is
making fun of the *artes praedicandi*, the manuals which gave
instructions on writing sermons, or that we should conclude that
what he says must be comic because the matter does not match
its formal frame. Medieval writers were acutely conscious of
formal units and patterned models, and a great many well-
known forms and formulae of religious origin, such as the Ten
Commandments, the Mass, the daily offices, the rite of con-
fession, various prayers, and so on, were adapted to profane
purposes. No doubt the religious parallel lent a certain extra
piquancy to some of the amorous material which was treated
in this way, but the use of a religious form for a profane but
serious purpose is not a clear indication for us to presuppose a
primarily humorous intention on the part of the author. There
are abundant modern instances of the adoption of the Decalogue
to such matters as how the visitor from the city should conduct
himself in the country, or how the courteous motorist should
behave, and their authors not only expect the content of these
codes to be taken seriously but have no thought of satirizing
the Ten Commandments. There *are* elements in the content of
San Pedro's *Sermon* which may cause us to doubt the seriousness of all he says, but they need to be looked at and judged
separately.

Superficially, it would seem that Diego de San Pedro has
been converted to that extreme view of love which has been
referred to since the nineteenth century as "courtly love."[5]
Although it has been defined in a number of different ways, the
set of notions habitually labeled as "courtly love" varies from
place to place and from period to period; but San Pedro has
got hold of at least four of the most widespread and characteristic ideas. One is that unrequited love is an extremely painful
experience which leads to physical illness and may ultimately
cause death; this idea was by no means confined to the poets,

and is expressed perfectly seriously in any number of medieval and Renaissance medical treatises (love being dealt with under the heading of mental illness).[6] A corollary of this idea, and one which appears to be almost a constant of the literature of love in a great many unrelated cultures—it is, after all, a very obvious one—is that the lady who has caused the pain may, if she chooses, cure it.[7]

However, although the love poets of the Middle Ages might be prepared to accept a "remedy" offered by the lady (and this might range from as little as her indicating that she did really believe that the poet was in love with her, through recip- rocated love, to sexual consummation), they were not prepared to accept other remedies prescribed by the doctors, or even to accept that there might be such remedies. Instead, they insisted on the value of love as a spiritual experience: love was not something to be avoided, and their suffering was good, worth- while, and ennobling of itself.

Furthermore, although love might stem from physical desire aroused by beauty, love was more than lust: it also involved spiritual adoration; the beauty and virtue and *rightness* of the beloved were unquestionable; the lover was to show her abso- lute devotion and total subservience to her wishes; if he were truly in love he should want only what his mistress wanted. Furthermore, since his beloved's welfare must be his prime concern, he must take the greatest care not to embarrass her in any way, and most especially not to say or do anything that might lead to her honor's being called into question.

There is nothing unusual about these ideas. There certainly existed a great many skeptics, of varied complexion, who thought that love was only a form of madness, who denied that there was any difference between love and lust, who poured scorn on the idea that there was such a thing as "true love" if that were to be defined as constant love, who refused to believe anyone could die of love, who thought women were inferior creatures, and so on; but there were nevertheless a number of people who did accept the basic ideas of "courtly love" with, apparently, complete conviction. Our problem is to determine whether, in writing his *Sermon,* Diego de San Pedro was one of the believers or not.

There is more than one element in his *Sermon* which does not seem quite to square with wholehearted conviction and sincerity. One is that he paints a ridiculous picture of the lover, especially in the third section. When he is urging the ladies to have compassion on their languishing swains, he describes the disorientation of their lovers in these terms:

In the ecstasy of contemplation of your beauty and virtue, they lose the wit to speak, and rationality to make reply; they do not know where they are going or where they have come from; they do not speak to the purpose, and they go about in a daze. In church, beside the altar, they ask if there is Mass; after they have risen from a meal, they ask if it is mealtime. How often it happens that a lover holds his food halfway between his mouth and his plate for a long space of time, not knowing in his bewilderment who is to eat it, he or the plate! When they are going to bed, they inquire if the sun has risen, and when they rise they ask if night has fallen.

What should have been a serious and sympathetic portrait of a man in love is undermined by the ludicrousness of the detail.

Again, while it is not absurd to suggest that a man could die of love nor to imply that true love means respecting the beloved's wishes, San Pedro puts these propositions in such exaggerated terms, taking it to the impossible extreme, laying down that a man should be willing to be damned if his mistress so wills it, that he brings into the open the conflict between this code of "courtly love" and religion itself. In *Prison of Love*, as we shall see, San Pedro is most careful to insist that, so far from there being any conflict between love and religion, love of a woman can lead a man to God. But here he presents his code of love as a flagrant contradiction of Christian duty.

Again, at the conclusion of his *Sermon*, San Pedro tells the story of Pyramus and Thisbe to set a moral example for the ladies. I have already indicated that the story of Pyramus and Thisbe presents problems. It had been taken (and was still taken by certain authors later in the sixteenth century) as a moral allegory (Pyramus as Christ, etc.), and as a simple moral tale illustrating the foolishness of rash and hasty action. San Pedro gets another, different moral out of it: that ladies should be kind to their lovers. It does not seem really to follow from the tale.

And it is legitimate for us to wonder whether the whole episode was actually intended to be as farcical as it appears.

Other absurdities in the *Sermon* include the obviously specious arguments by which San Pedro convicts disdainful ladies of the four mortal sins of Pride, Anger, Avarice, and Sloth. But in reality these arguments are hardly more specious or absurd than some of those which, in *Prison of Love,* Leriano on his death-bed is to use in his defense of women. It is something in the tone of the whole context which leads us to treat the arguments of the *Sermon* with a certain wariness, suspecting a leg-pull. That final mention of *gloria* is enough to stop short anyone who has any acquaintance with fifteenth-century Spanish love poetry.

But if there is some element of clowning in the *Sermon,* if San Pedro dons his motley to amuse the ladies of the court, there is nevertheless more than a residue of seriousness in what he says. We can see, from looking at his two very different courtly romances, that he is in process of moving from the attitude and ideas which we find in *Arnalte and Lucenda* to what we find in *Prison of Love. Arnalte and Lucenda,* rather like the *Sermon,* has its ambiguous, Ovidian, comic moments. On the other hand, we can see from the precepts set out in the *Sermon,* even ignoring some of the more extreme rules, how far and how frequently Arnalte offended against the code: taking no precautions to keep his passion secret, importuning and embarrassing the woman he professes to love, insisting that Lucenda owes him favors, rushing headlong into violent action in a transport of anger and jealousy, taking no account of her wishes, and so on. Moreover, we shall see that in *Prison of Love* the basic precepts of the *Sermon* are treated with complete gravity, that Leriano is a perfect lover, that there is nothing comic about the novel, and that there is no ambiguity about its message. One quite fundamental issue on which San Pedro was to make up his mind was the question of feminism: whether he was to place himself among those who preached that women were in every way inferior to men, weak, timorous, vain, foolish, given to back-biting gossip, and sinful, or among those who held that (if I may paraphrase) all the gentler virtues of a humane, cultured, and civilized society were due to the influence of women.

CHAPTER 7

Cárcel de Amor (Prison of Love)

I *The Story*

SUPERFICIALLY, the story of *Prison of Love* bears some resemblance to the story of *Arnalte and Lucenda*. It opens once more with the narrator journeying through a wilderness, returning through the Sierra Morena, in fact, to spend the winter at home after the summer's fighting (presumably in the war against Granada). Suddenly, in a dark and narrow valley he comes upon a strange apparition. A ferocious knight dressed in skins carries a sculptured figurine of a woman of extraordinary beauty, and flames emanating from this image envelop and draw irresistibly after it a groaning captive who begs the Author to help him. Not without fear and misgiving, the Author accosts the formidable savage, who informs him that he is Desire, chief officer of Love, and that he is taking his captive to Love's Prison.[1] The apparition then vanishes, leaving the Author lost in the mountains as night falls. But at daybreak he perceives on the highest peak of the mountain range the huge glistening tower of the Prison, of mysterious and complex structure, makes his way there, enters, and finds the captive in the topmost room of the tower, chained, seated in a chair of fire, and being subjected to sundry exotic tortures, including crowning with a crown of metal spikes.

The captive then explains these mysteries to the astonished Author. He is Leriano, son of the late Duke Guersio and the Duchess Coleria, of the kingdom of Macedonia, and he has fallen in love with Laureola, daughter of King Gaulo. His jail is the Prison of Love, the foundations of which are made of Constant Love; the four sustaining columns are his Reason, Understanding, Memory, and Will; the guards and the torturers are Sadness, Anguish, Misfortune, Despair, Passion, Pain, Suffering, and so on. Each minute detail has its allegorical explanation.

96

The Author is relieved to hear that the Prison is the creation of Leriano's infatuation (*enamorada condición*) and not the construct of some diabolical magic, and agrees to help him by telling Laureola of the state in which he has found him. He duly makes his way to the court at Suria, and after a few days meets Laureola and gains her interest by recounting the marvelous things to be found in Spain. At last finding her alone, he takes the opportunity to tell her of Leriano's sorry state, and to say that all Leriano asks is that she should feel some compassion for him (speech). Laureola is outraged and tells the Author that if he had been a Macedonian she would have had him executed, and threatens him with death if he should raise the subject again (speech).

The Author, however, resolves that he will, if necessary, put his life at risk for Leriano's sake, and stays at court. Seeing that Laureola treats him as though nothing had happened, he wonders whether this is an invitation to him to reopen the subject, and with a show of feigned terror does so. This time Laureola is equally harsh in her words, but less so in her manner, and the Author subsequently seizes every chance to talk to her about Leriano until he thinks he perceives signs of her being affected: pensive, avoiding company, sighing, blushing. He mistakes these symptoms, as he at once informs us, for love, when they are no more than indications of her softheartedness (*piedad*), and decides, therefore, misguidedly, to return to Leriano and persuade him to write Laureola a letter.

Leriano accordingly himself sets out in writing (the letter is given in full) his devotion to Laureola and his readiness to die for her, and describes the acuteness of his suffering, begging her to write him a letter which will ease his pain. The Author carries the letter to Laureola and hands it over with a speech in which he emphasizes the noble selflessness of Leriano's love, and begs her to save his life by receiving his letter and replying to it. Laureola explains to the Author (speech) that there is no way in which she can help Leriano without compromising her honor, and blames herself for having allowed this private relationship to progress even thus far. But she accepts the letter. The Author, now thoroughly confused, returns to Leriano, tells him of the contradictions in Laureola's behavior, urges him to put his faith in his own constancy, and offers to continue to assist him in any way he can (speech).

Leriano says that he understands the contradictions imposed by considerations of honor, tells the Author that he has himself chosen an honorable death, and asks him as a final favor to take a letter of farewell to Laureola (speech). In this letter Leriano writes that he could never have contemplated anything which might prejudice Laureola's reputation, can find no reason or justification for her condemning him to death, and insists that the first and last reward (*galardón*) which he would have asked of her was a reply to his letter. Now he asks only that she give him the consolation of knowing, when he has gone to that place where despairing souls go, that she will "honor his bones."

The Author hands over the letter, and on the following day Laureola, disturbed, embarrassed, blushing, and breathless, hands to him the reply she has written to Leriano. In it she writes of the conflict between her compassion and her fear for her reputation, and declares that her reply has been prompted only by pity and not by love. But the Author is overjoyed, and, accompanied by a force which includes Hope, Joy, Contentment, and Pleasure, returns to the Prison and puts to flight Leriano's jailers.

Leriano, after a brief convalescence, returns to the court, and kisses Laureola's hand. The Author, aware of their relationship, observes that both are disturbed and tongue-tied. But so does Persio, a noble friend of Leriano, who has fallen in love with Laureola, and, maddened by jealousy, he denounces Leriano and Laureola to the King, swearing to what he only suspects: that they are spending the nights together. The King forthwith commits Laureola to prison, and orders Persio to accuse Leriano of treason and challenge him to trial by combat. The letters of challenge and reply (given in full) are duly exchanged; the fight takes place; and Leriano, having cut off Persio's right hand, is about to kill him when the King, pressed by members of Persio's family, intervenes to save his life. Leriano protests (speech), but the King refuses to come to a hasty decision, and the delay gives Persio the chance to suborn three witnesses to confirm the truth of his allegations. The King, ignoring the outcome of the trial by combat, condemns Laureola to death for adultery. Leriano, in an access of passion, determines at once to free Laureola and kill Persio, but the Author advises him of the indiscretion of such an act, warns him of the risk of failure, and counsels other measures designed to safeguard Laureola's honor (speech).

Leriano sees the sense of the Author's disinterested advice, and agrees to try other remedies. But first he writes to Laureola to tell her not to be afraid, for he will save her (letter). The Author, under cover of darkness, pushes the letter into her cell, and next morning finds a reply from her, and receives a brief word from her as he picks it up: "You see the reward I have received for being compassionate." The letter (given in full) amplifies her complaint, tells of the torture to which she is being subjected, and begs him to save not her life, but her honor.

The Author decides that it is wiser to withhold this letter from Leriano, and himself sets about organizing those who believe in Laureola's innocence to protest on her behalf. The Cardinal makes a speech about the duties of kingship, royal obligation to take counsel, the dangers of hasty action, the virtue of mercy, the manifest innocence of the Princess, and the known wickedness of the three witnesses. The King rejects this advice, and alleges that his honor is more important than his daughter's life (speech). The Author persuades the Queen to appeal to her husband, but she has no more success, and goes to visit her daughter and weep over her imminent death (lament). The Author gets a message to Laureola to urge her to make her own appeal to the King, and she writes a letter (given in full) declaring her innocence and expressing her concern for her father's reputation: for a king falls into disrepute by the exercise of cruelty and not by clemency. The King, however, is adamant, and the Author approaches Laureola's uncle, Galio, to set in train the plans for the rescue of Laureola by force: Galio agrees to protect his niece's honor by taking her under his protection as soon as Leriano frees her.

Only at this point does the Author return to Leriano and give him Laureola's letter, and though Leriano is thrown into a turmoil of emotion, he is prevailed upon to set about organizing the rescue. Plans are duly laid, and put into action at dawn on the day of the execution. Leriano and his men attack the jail and

release Laureola while one of his captains seeks out and kills
Persio. Galio takes charge of his niece and conducts her to his
own fortress of Dala, and Leriano and his troops beat a strategic retreat to Leriano's fortress of Susa, to which the King
and his army soon lay siege.

The rigorous siege lasts three months, during which Leriano
is wounded and loses the greater part of his men. Knowing
that the royal army is about to launch another full-scale assault,
he delivers a harangue (given in full), and in the ensuing conflict three thousand of the King's fifty thousand men are killed,
and Leriano's own troops are reduced to 150. But to demonstrate
that he is far from defeated, he sends out fifty men to attack
one of the besieging posts which he knows to be manned by
members of Persio's family, and they capture one of the false
witnesses who testified against Laureola. Leriano orders him
to be tortured, but the man confesses at once; Leriano informs
the King, who lifts the siege, executes all three witnesses, and
receives Laureola back at court with great ceremony and tears
of joy. But Leriano, to his chagrin, is ordered to stay away from
the court until his erstwhile enemies have been appeased, and
he at once relapses into his former state. He begs the Author
to find some way for him to see and speak to Laureola, and the
Author persuades him to write her a letter.

In the letter Leriano tells Laureola that he is once more dying
for love of her and that only some compassionate act of hers
can save him, and asks that she say specifically whether she
wants him to die, so that he may know he is fulfilling her wishes.
Laureola replies that she does feel extremely sorry for him,
and that that is the only reward she can give; she is very deeply
in his debt, and when she inherits the kingdom she will demonstrate her gratitude by loading him with every honor; but she
cannot and will not speak with him or permit any continuation
of their relationship, for that would confirm in the minds of
the populace the truth of the accusation of which she has just
been acquitted.

The Author returns to Leriano and advises him that there
is nothing left for him but to die. Leriano is profoundly grate-
ful to the Author for his honest friendship, agrees that this is
the last service he can perform for Laureola, takes to his bed,

and refuses food and drink. A close friend of Leriano, a knight named Tefeo, guesses that Leriano has been brought to this pass through unrequited love (though he does not suspect Laureola), and to rally his friend begins to abuse the entire female sex, citing all the examples he can think of to illustrate the worthlessness of women. (San Pedro disposes of this in three or four lines, not repeating Tefeo's speech.) Leriano, incensed, embarks on a long defense of women, giving fifteen reasons for condemning men who speak ill of women, twenty reasons why men are indebted to women, and finally a catalogue of examples of virtuous women. The effort, however, leaves him at the point of death.

His mother, the Duchess Coleria, having been alarmed by sundry omens, comes to see Leriano and finds him dying. She pronounces a lament, enumerating his many virtues, protesting against the inequity of Death, wishing that Leriano had been of grosser fibre, insensitive and unintelligent, and bewails her own fate.

Leriano regains consciousness and remembers Laureola's letters. He hesitates to destroy them, but dares not leave them in anyone else's hands, so he shreds them and drinks them in a cup of water. He then pronounces the words: *Acabados son mis males,* words strikingly close to those with which San Pedro in *The Passion* renders the dying Christ's "It is finished" (*Acabados son mis dolores y amarguras*). And so, comments the Author, his death became a witness to his "faith," the constancy of his love. Having attended his funeral, the Author, heartbroken, makes his unwilling way back to Peñafiel.

Once more it must be noted, as with *Arnalte and Lucenda,* that a summary of the plot of the novel gives a misleading impression. Numerous incidents are disposed of in swift chapters of close-packed narrative, and what takes up the space is again the letters and speeches, which are given verbatim. (See Chapter 5, Section II: "Narrative and discourse.")

II Prison of Love *and* Arnalte and Lucenda

There are various obvious resemblances between *Prison of Love* and *Arnalte and Lucenda*; Menéndez Pelayo, indeed, described *Arnalte and Lucenda* as a "first draft" (*primer esbozo*) of *Prison of Love*, and Diego de San Pedro was himself well aware that *Prison of Love* was not dissimilar from some of his earlier work, for in the prologue addressed to the Alcaide de los Donceles, he writes: "It is possible that I shall be criticized for repeating here things which I have already written in other works."[2] But, as San Pedro must also have known, the differences between *Prison of Love* and *Arnalte and Lucenda* are profound, and they are much more interesting and important than the similarities.

The story opens in exactly the same way as in *Arnalte and Lucenda*, with the narrator wandering through a wilderness, but almost at once, and in striking contrast with the initial here-and-now setting of time and place (in the Sierra Morena, after the summer campaign against Granada), we find ourselves in a world of allegory, which occupies a substantial number of pages and two "chapters" of the narrative.

We find echoes of *Arnalte* again when, after a meal, the love-stricken hero begins to explain his plight to the astonished Author. But in *Arnalte* the story is all in the past, and again San Pedro departs from his own precedent, by making himself, "the Author," an active participant in a far from completed tale.

Moving on, we find once more the by now familiar letters and speeches; the narrator makes his speech to Laureola following the same rhetorical formulae employed in *Arnalte*; Laureola responds in like fashion; and there is still no dialogue. But what we do find is a greater number of letters, so that San Pedro moves a step further toward the epistolary novel, and also a greater variety of rhetorical set pieces, for not all the speeches or letters are concerned with the love affair. We have two mothers' laments (technically the medieval *planctus*), the political discourses of the King and the Cardinal, a harangue, etc.

We know from the very beginning of Leriano's explanations that he is in love with a Princess, and that he himself is the son of a Duke (presumably, indeed, a Duke himself, though the author never makes this clear). Although *Arnalte and Lucenda* has a court setting, we are now still higher up the social scale, which gives greater dignity (according to medieval theory and according to Aristotle) to the whole story, for the fate of a kingdom now hangs in the balance. Moreover, the relative social status of Leriano and Laureola is plain: she is his superior, whereas, since we have no information about the rank of Arnalte and Lucenda, we must presume them to be equal. The superiority of the lady, and the consequent inferiority and suppliant posture of her servitor, are more in accord with the traditions of "courtly love." It is even dangerous for Leriano to approach Laureola at all. As he observes in his first letter to her, she could have him put to death, and we have already seen her threatening the Author with execution. Leriano's love, therefore, is doubly a threat to his own life and so the more praiseworthy.

The crisis is also much better contrived. It is brought on by the jealousy and suspicion of the false knight, Persio, and Leriano is almost wholly blameless.[3] Once more we have the episode of judicial combat, with the letters of challenge and reply again given in full, and the description of the fight again shortened.[4] But this time it is the false friend who makes the accusation and the hero who repudiates it.

The termination of the combat by the King, before Persio can be killed (there is still, perhaps, a slight weakness in the plotting here),[5] is a further variation from the "first draft" which opens up new areas as Persio goes on to further machinations. The condemnation of Laureola to death for adultery (a penalty which did exist in some ancient and early medieval codes, and which is a device also used by Juan de Flores)[6] brings in some wholly new elements: a diplomatic episode and a military episode. The narrator first puts into operation his scheme for saving Laureola by diplomatic means (the appeals by the Cardinal, the Queen, and the Princess herself), and when these possibilities are exhausted, aids Leriano in planning and executing the attack on the jail, the strategic retreat, and the resistance to the siege.

The final rejection of the lover by his beloved is also fundamentally different from the similar situation in the earlier story. In *Arnalte*, Lucenda retires to a convent, mourning her husband and believing Arnalte to be her enemy (she tells the abbess that she has not entered her convent to be molested by the sister of her *enemigo*).[7] But Laureola is deeply grieved for Leriano, offers him any reward he might wish when she becomes Queen, and withholds no more than personal intimacy, and that only because she cannot afford to put her reputation at risk again. Moreover, Leriano accepts this decision completely, makes no attempt to dissuade her, and regards it as final and irrevocable.

Another substantial section new in *Prison of Love* and without precedent in *Arnalte and Lucenda* is the dying Leriano's lengthy defense of women, provoked by the attempt of Tefeo to divert him from his course. It has been criticized as a tedious and irrelevant digression. But in fifteenth-century Spain, the feminist debate, though it reached its peak earlier,[8] was still a live issue of some moment, and San Pedro, through Leriano, makes his position clear. Unlike Juan de Flores, who in *Grisel and Mirabella* gives both sides of the argument (indeed the antifeminist champion Torrellas wins the debate),[9] San Pedro reports in a few unspecific words what Tefeo has to say, *díxole infinitos males de las mugeres* ("he spoke all manner of evil of womankind"),[10] and devotes his space to an impassioned profeminist statement. It would not have been in any way tedious for his contemporary audience. Furthermore, in a novel of this nature it has a clear function in complementing the initial allegory, for in it Leriano argues—as the allegory does when Understanding and Reason consent to Leriano's imprisonment—that since women are, through the power of love, the source of all the gentle arts and a stimulus to virtue, love is a valuable, reasonable, noble, and ennobling emotion. It is also highly relevant to the plot and the theme of the novel in that it at once justifies Leriano's martyrdom and contributes to the portrait of the perfect lover.

And, not quite finally, we have the lament of Leriano's mother, which some critics have found of a "moving simplicity."[11] I think this misses the subtlety of San Pedro's handling of this piece and misleads us as to his purpose. Certainly the burden of Coleria's complaint is that she is to be left bereaved, to drag out her days alone. But, first of all, she wishes that Leriano had been some crude peasant, insensitive and unintelligent, who would not have been susceptible to passion; and this is an obviously unacceptable alternative. And, secondly, the Duchess

is not given the last word, for Leriano is not dead, and can rally
to think yet once more of safeguarding Laureola's reputation,
and to accept death with dignified resignation. It may not be a
happy ending, but we are left convinced that his death was
inevitable, noble, worthy of a perfect lover, and certainly not
unacceptable to the martyr of love.

Some of these elements new in *Prison of Love* deserve closer
examination.

III   *The Allegory*

The allegory at the beginning of the novel is a very important
new departure for San Pedro, and in its context it performs a
number of important functions. This ancient device, of which
there are innumerable medieval examples,[12] was clearly much
to the taste of the writers of the early Renaissance; but it is not
very helpful, in trying to explain its presence and function in
Prison of Love, merely to say that it appealed to contemporary
taste.

One of the things it does is to provide a concrete model of
a psychological theory of love and at the same time a series of
statements justifying passion and an implicit set of rules for the
constant lover's conduct. Without writing another treatise or
sermon on the subject, San Pedro has conveyed his ideas through
a plastic, symbolic representation of them. (No doubt, for his
earlier readers there was also a certain pleasure in guessing at
the meaning of the symbols in the first "chapter" before reach-
ing the explanations in the second.) He shows how love is
born, what happens to the various faculties of the soul when a
man "falls in love," justifies its rationality by having Understanding and Reason consent, affirms that true love is ever constant
("Love is not love / Which alters when it alteration finds"),[13]
and even predicts the probable outcome, when Reason condemns Leriano to death.

But it also sets the tone of the whole story. The very fact
that it opens with an allegorical introduction was an indication
that this was to be an artistic, solemn, and uplifting work;[14] but
it affects the atmosphere of the novel in another way, for there
is a reason-defying transition from "perfect allegory" through

"imperfect allegory" to the real world.[15] At the start San Pedro uses what the medieval theorists termed "perfect allegory," an allegory in which, that is, apart from the names of Desire and Love, we are given no clue to the interpretation of the vision. (What is the shining eagle on the summit of the tower? Who is the Negro who strikes at Leriano with a halberd?) But we then move into a world of "imperfect allegory" (or personification) in which abstract entities are known by their names, and from this move mysteriously from Spain to Macedonia.[16] Furthermore, after his first visit to the court at Suria, the Author returns to the allegorical Prison accompanied by allegorical troops. Although it is wrong to say that the whole romance is allegorical,[17] and although modern readers may object to the failure to draw a clear-cut line between the world of ideas and the world of objects, San Pedro, by blurring the boundaries, has conferred upon the whole romance something of the quality of a dream (some might say a nightmare), and in his at once real and unreal Macedonian setting he is free to tell his extraordinary idealized story without allowing mundane detail or further objection to intrude.

IV *The Author*

The introduction of the Author as an active participant in the action brings to *Prison of Love* a dimension which was lacking in *Arnalte and Lucenda*.[18] The Author is, of course, essential because this particular tale cannot be told in the first person, for the very simple reason that the protagonist is not in the end left alive to recount his spiritual adventure. But this has important consequences. While in *Arnalte* we have only the simple and ancient device of a tale-within-a-tale, in *Prison of Love* Leriano's story is by no means finished when he has finished recounting it to the Author. The Author is very much involved in the action and is to some degree responsible for what happens. Given the premises that true love is by definition constant and that unrequited love eventually kills, he could not have averted the tragedy of Leriano's death, but, having helped to put Laureola in peril, he does contribute substantially to saving her life and her honor by restraining Leriano from foolhardy action at the moment of crisis and by advising Leriano on the possible ways of saving her.

The Author, by becoming involved in the action himself, ceases to be the omniscient author of, for instance, the romances of chivalry. He can be confused or deceived, as he is by misinterpreting Laureola's reactions to his pressing of Leriano's suit; and he is by no means neutral. He keeps up, in the narrative links, a running commentary on his reactions to the development of the situation, and by his expressions of admiration and sympathy for Leriano we are left in little doubt about how San Pedro intended us to react.

However, since the main love story is told by the Author and not the enamored hero, we do have in *Prison of Love* an outside observer, if not a completely impartial one. He can stand aside when Leriano's judgment is impaired by rage and offer cool counsel; and since he does have this detached role, we know also what we are to think of Laureola. Although the Author, after accepting her final letter for Leriano and his own dismissal—he too is banished, because his private conversations with her are arousing curiosity—abandons himself to extremities of grief on his return journey, weeping and crying aloud, his distress is his only reaction to Laureola's decision: he does not query it or call her cruel, and himself advises Leriano that now his only remedy is death. He provides good evidence that the critics who have seen Laureola as an archetypal *belle dame sans merci* are as sadly astray as were some of San Pedro's contemporaries, or Hans Ludwig von Kufstein, the German translator, who renamed her Rigorosa.[19]

The relationship between the Author and the author, Diego de San Pedro, is a curious one. Clearly the romance is in no way genuinely autobiographical (or for that matter based on fact at all), and for the purpose of the narrative the author assumes the persona of *el Autor*. But how far does the fictitious "I" of the romance represent the writer? There is no evidence that Diego de San Pedro, even if he were of the gentry (an *hidalgo*), possessed the status to converse intimately with a princess, or even to be the confidant of a duke. In raising the social status of Leriano and Laureola, San Pedro has raised his own status. Moreover, the diplomatic and military episodes are a little odd, for while they extend the complications of the plot, they are not structurally essential and could have been dismissed in a few brief lines. It is Diego de San Pedro, perhaps, secretary to the Count of Urueña, who is here endeavoring to demonstrate that he has both diplomatic ability and military experience; for it should be noted that the three phases of the military campaign, the raid, the retreat, the siege, are quite certainly not, as some critics would have it, relics of San Pedro's adherence to the tradition of the chivalric romance, but a realistic account of the kind of warfare which was being waged in contemporary Granada. San Pedro as *el Autor* displays himself as someone he might have been. It fits with what we can deduce about his personality.

V *The Perfect Lover and the Perfect Lady*

It is not particularly fruitful to talk of the "characters" of Leriano and Laureola: each is an idealized type. What we can say about Leriano is little more than what we can say about the type of the perfect lover. It is true that from time to time we learn of details which turn him into a specific individual: he has a mother, but his father is dead, and he is twenty years old (a round figure which emerges only toward the end of the story, in the Duchess's lament, and which may not be intended to be exact); but everything else that we know about him tends to be nonspecific. He is a "Macedonian," but Macedonia is such a vague and unreal country (to which, it seems, one travels much like Alice to Wonderland) that this serves to "departicularize" rather than particularize him: his Macedonian nationality identifies him as an individual less than if he had been described as German or French or Spanish. That he is of noble birth is part also of the essential picture, for as Leriano's mother says, and as the doctors acknowledge, it is only noble and sensitive souls who are susceptible to the dangerous passion of love.[20] And it should not surprise us that the perfect lover is the perfect courtier, and hence skilled at arms as well as in letters,[21] and, inevitably, not only a redoubtable duelist, but a shrewd military strategist.

There is a vast distance between Arnalte and Leriano, for

the languishing lover of *Arnalte and Lucenda* has become the irreproachable lover. The crisis which endangers Laureola's life is not essentially Leriano's fault, and he repeatedly risks his own life in order to save hers, first in the duel with Persio, and then in the raid on the jail, and, since Laureola has gained only a temporary haven at Dala, in the continued engagement with the royal forces. Arnalte does nothing comparable, and, even if he does believe Lucenda to have been an unwilling bride,[22] fights his duel for his own reasons, to avenge the treachery of Elierso, and without attempting to ascertain what Lucenda might want.

Leriano, again unlike Arnalte, but exactly like Amadís-Beltenebrós in *Amadís de Gaula* (*Amadis of Gaul,* or, possibly, *of Wales*),[23] not only has himself no reproaches for the lady who has rejected him, but refuses to permit anyone else to criticize her in any way, not even in the indirect way in which Tefeo maligns the entire female sex. He idealizes not only his own beloved Laureola, but, through her, all women, and the uplifting power of love.

Finally, Leriano does actually die of love. When the Author comes across Arnalte, he is merely awaiting death, still cherishing a rather vague hope, and is ready to publish his story so that he may at least receive the solace of knowing that other, gentle ladies will sympathize with his misfortunes. We cannot know how long Arnalte will put up with his existence in the wilderness or whether some other lady will not take Lucenda's place (as Dante, after the death of Beatrice, found comfort in speaking to other women about love, and eventually found one to replace her).[24] But, as the Author notes, Leriano's death bore witness to his constant love; and perhaps only his death, gladly accepted without any reproach for Laureola, could be the final proof of perfect love.

Leriano is a martyr who is glad to die for his "faith," and there is more than one hint that Leriano is, like Christ, martyred for sins which are not his own. The image is suggested in the initial allegory, with the iron "crown of thorns," and impresses itself upon the reader even more irresistibly when Leriano drinks the last cup and pronounces: "It is finished." But it is possible that Diego de San Pedro, even at this stage, felt a little uneasy about Leriano's fate. Despite the way in which Leriano, or San Pedro, insists on the compatibility of passionate love and love of God (he even affirms that love leads men to the three theological virtues of Faith, Hope, and Charity, as well as to the four cardinal virtues), and despite the fact that several of his examples of virtuous women are suicides (not only from pagan classical history, but from recent Spanish history), Leriano himself suggests, in the letter to Laureola which finally provokes her to reply, that he is due to go where despairing souls go.[25] It is not clear, after all that has happened in the interval, and in his resigned acceptance of his death, that the situation has radically changed. In his *Sermon,* San Pedro preached that perfect lovers should be prepared to accept the torments of the damned; but Leriano's defense of love as a way to God perhaps indicates that he had changed his mind. Possibly San Pedro meant to imply that the fulfillment of Leriano's martyrdom had saved him from Hell; but Nicolás Núñez was perhaps a better theologian when he has the ghost of Leriano emerge pale and sorrowful from the shades and be recalled at the first sign of daylight by a doleful summons.[26]

Nor is it entirely clear what Leriano wanted, or would have wanted ultimately from Laureola.[27] Arnalte is unequivocal: he wishes to marry Lucenda (although it is true that he thinks of it only after Elierso has done so and he has made her a widow). But we do not know where Leriano's requests would have ended. Initially all he wants is that Laureola should know that he is in love with her and suffering "for her sake"; but after she has been informed of this by the Author (who, wiser than Leriano, begs her to afford him some relief), Leriano wants an endorsement from Laureola of the existence of some special relationship between them and asks for a letter from her in reply; and after the external events of the false accusation and Leriano's acting as her savior have effectively interwoven the patterns of their lives, he wants again to see and speak with her. Here, this game of changing rules is brought to an abrupt halt when Laureola reaches her logical and unalterable decision to terminate the relationship. The appetite of love grows by what it feeds on and knows no surfeit until some climax is achieved. We can believe that Leriano would never have been guilty of conduct unworthy of an ideal courtier and perfect lover, but can we realistically believe that he would have remained content merely to see Laureola and talk with her from time to time? Leriano was led behind the hairy savage Desire by the flames emanating from a figurine of a woman of extraordinary beauty. Would his posture of adoration have made her untouchable?

This is a central problem in the whole debate about "courtly love." Andrew the Chaplain advises against *amor mixtus*, that is, love which admits sexual consummation, and prefers *amor purus*, where desire is kept at fever pitch by, for instance, kissing, embracing, viewing, and touching the beloved's nude body, without any climactic release,[28] but he is forced to concede that fulfilled sexual love is also *verus amor* ("true love"). It is, however, abundantly clear that any number of poets did not share his views. Many, and possibly a majority, saw sexual union as the logical and natural end of their desires—while insisting that love, implying respect and affection for the beloved, was far removed from lust. Others again may well have discovered satisfaction and the glow of virtue in distant adoration and uplifting abstinence. There are, quite simply, all shades of opinion to be found. But, in the case of San Pedro, we cannot really say what he believed when he wrote *Prison of Love*, for he has not provided us with the evidence to give a firm answer.

Laureola is a figure perhaps even less particularized than Leriano. We have no portrait of her; we do not know her age; and it could even be contended that we do not know what she really feels. While some critics have maintained that she is in love with Leriano, others have called her ungrateful and cruel.[29] Nicolás Núñez continued the story by having the Author find her bitterly repentant of her folly (she had not believed Leriano would really die) and having her confess to him that she had been in love with Leriano. But this continuation has made a quite different story of *Prison of Love*: it has become as foolish and needless a tragedy as the story of Pyramus and Thisbe or Romeo and Juliet; and in San Pedro's text as it stands there is no justification for this interpretation. While her lover would obviously adjudge Laureola faultless, the Author too has no criticism to make of her or of her conduct. It is true

that if the Author tells us he was mistaken when he believed
that Laureola was in love with Leriano we are not bound
to believe him, because he is not an omniscient author and
he confesses his own confusion at what seems her contradictory
words and behavior; but we really need more evidence than
we have to affirm that Laureola loved Leriano. Since the Author
does not blame her, since we are in an ideal realm of idealized
figures, and since we know what San Pedro believed to be the
supreme feminine virtue—compassion—we must conclude that
Laureola feels no more than acute compassion for Leriano,
accompanied by almost equally acute embarrassment in speaking of it at all. Her rejection of her lover, as of the company
of the Author, springs not from cruelty or ingratitude, but from
the highest consideration of all, her honor. It is the first and
fundamental rule in the code for lovers which San Pedro sets
out in the *Sermon*: the lover's foremost consideration must
be for his beloved's reputation.

One could argue that Leriano is a martyr to the latent malice
of the populace, those grosser spirits who always believe the
worst, and are incapable of appreciating refinement of feeling.[30]
Both he and Laureola are, in their different ways, victims of the
same harsh law of honor which became the mainspring of many
a Golden Age tragedy; Laureola is, indeed, almost a victim of
that even harsher "law of Scotland" which condemned her to
death.[31] But it was surely not San Pedro's intention to assail
the contemporary concern for honor, and even less the barbaric
but long defunct medieval code by which adulterous women
were executed. The conflict between love and honor is not a
conflict between two different ways of viewing one's obliga-
tions,[32] for the perfect lover must be honorable, and his first
concern must be for the honor of his beloved. Laureola, with
whatever regrets, and however much pity she may feel for
Leriano, has no choice: she must choose her honor. She would
not have been worthy of Leriano's love if she had not done so.
Leriano could be said to have chosen *both* love *and* honor, his
own and Laureola's, despite the fact that this involves his
choosing death. The risk was there when he embarked on his
spiritual adventure, and he had the misfortune to love a woman
ideal in every way, one who *was* moved to compassion, but

who would be unable, because of very special circumstances, to offer him any relief or reward.

VI *Style*

One of the many not inconsiderable merits of *Prison of Love* is its style, which has been widely if sometimes rather vaguely praised: "elegant," Menéndez Pelayo called it. Gili Gaya felt that it was preferable to the style of *Arnalte and Lucenda,* and attributes the improvement to San Pedro's growing maturity as a writer.

There are several important points to make clear here. First, *Prison of Love* is in no way "less rhetorical" than *Arnalte and Lucenda,* and the only specifically rhetorical devices which San Pedro either ceases to employ or employs only rarely are half a dozen, of the forty-odd "colors of rhetoric," which have been identified as "acoustic conceits." (See Chapter 5, Section VIII: "The style of *Arnalte and Lucenda.*") He also abandons his Latinizing syntax. San Pedro himself, in his prefatory remarks, explains why he did so: "because I was told I should write some work in the style of a discourse which I sent to Doña Marina Manuel, for she thought it was less bad than the style I used in another romance of mine that she looked at."[33] The preferred style was the style of his *Sermon,* a fairly straight-forward piece of Spanish prose, in which the only unnatural feature is the continued use of a subjunctive after *como;* and clearly San Pedro must have adopted that relatively simple style because it seemed to him more suited to a vernacular sermon. But the explanation he gives of his stylistic reform is not entirely adequate, for the style of *Prison of Love* is not the style of the *Sermon,* and San Pedro could not have achieved the results he did with so very vague a directive.

The difference between the rhetoric of *Arnalte and Lucenda* and the rhetoric of *Prison of Love* is the difference between medieval and Renaissance humanist rhetoric.[34] Devices which the classical rhetoricians had advised must be used very spar-ingly, and examples which were held up as horrible warnings rather than as models for imitation, found their way into medie-val manuals without the qualifications, and were enthusiastically adopted by medieval writers. The Italian humanists rediscovered the real Cicero and recovered the lost books of Quintilian. Moreover, Italian and Italian-trained scholars like Nebrija deplored the attempts to imitate the syntax of Latin in a language which was not Latin and lacked its resources. The phrase "good taste" (*buen gusto*) originated at the court of Isabella, and, though vague enough to admit of various interpretations, always signified a certain dignity and moderation. That San Pedro was not merely responding to such a generalized expression of taste, but restudying his rhetoric in some humanist manual, seems indicated by his use in *Prison of Love* of a whole category of rhetorical devices which are not to be found in *Arnalte and Lucenda* and which the medieval theorists show little interest in, namely the techniques of *abbreviatio*.[35]

There is, unfortunately, no real shortcut to the study of medieval rhetorical doctrine, and so to the proper description and comprehension of precisely what San Pedro was about in writing *Arnalte and Lucenda* and *Prison of Love*. It embraced much more than style, and concerned itself with the content of a discourse and how a writer could find his material (this is *inventio*, of which there are many methods); it was concerned with propriety and *decorum*, concepts which took in both the whole theory of style's being adjusted to the right level for the matter, or, if appropriate, for the speaker, as well as notions of verisimilitude somewhat different from our modern ones; it concerned itself with the proper purpose of literature: to instruct while delighting, properly to apportion praise and blame, and so forth. Rhetorical doctrine, that is, covers every aspect of composition in prose or verse and goes into every aspect of every problem in extraordinary detail.

So far as the disposition of a work is concerned, medieval doctrine (as I hinted in Chapter 5, Section II) tends to concern itself with the organization of small units, which are often very rigorously defined, and to lose sight of the larger unit. Medieval works are notoriously "bitty" and when they hang together at all they tend to do so within a grand framework which permits the insertion of "bits," as in Dante's *Divina Commedia*, the collections of tales made by Boccaccio, Chaucer, and Juan Manuel, or the Archpriest of Hita's *Book of Good Love*.

San Pedro's achievement in welding into a remarkably coherent work the various minor units (*narratio*, letters, speeches, *planctus*, harangue, *argumentatio*,[36] etc.) has been undervalued.

One underlying assumption throughout classical and medieval rhetorical theory, an assumption of the utmost importance, is that there are always right and wrong ways of doing something even if there is not always a clearly indicated *best* way. Variations are permitted, and different theorists will disagree on points of detail, but the broad assumption is that the writer must learn his craft and write correctly after a study both of the rules of the manuals and of the best models. The idea of a writer's having an original, a personal style simply never enters into the calculations of the rhetoricians.[37] Writing is, or ought to be, fine writing, and should follow the rules.

So far as what we now understand by "style" is concerned, there is one category of rhetorical techniques which is crucial for the proper comprehension and description of what San Pedro was doing in *Arnalte and Lucenda* and *Prison of Love*, and that is known as *amplificatio*.[38] While it was generally agreed that there were eight methods of *amplificatio*, different theorists arrived at the same total with different classifications, and many of these main methods, such as *expolitio, apostrophe*, or *comparatio*, contained numerous divisions and subdivisions which it would be impossible to list and illustrate here. I can say only that every one of the eight major methods of *amplificatio*, and most of the divisions and subdivisions, can be illustrated from the works of San Pedro.

We may, however, take notice of just three, which are of special importance at the purely stylistic level and which account for a great many of the figures which modern critics lump together as "antithetical" or "parallelistic." One is *interpretatio* (sometimes a division of *expolitio*) which involves saying the same thing in synonymous or near-synonymous terms. It is one of the most elementary ways of "amplifying" a discourse and it is not surprising to find that it is extremely frequent in *Arnalte and Lucenda* and somewhat less so in the more subtle *Prison of Love*. When Arnalte exclaims to himself, *¡O morada de desdichas! ¡O edificio de trabajos!* ("Oh, dwelling place of misfortune! Oh, home of sorrows!"), he is using *interpretatio*. Slightly more sophisticated is a formula of preference, "this rather than that," which is San Pedro's favorite amplifying formula, and another division of *expolitio*. When San Pedro writes, at the beginning of the prologue to *Prison of Love, Cuánto me estaría mejor preciarme de lo que callase que arrepentirme de lo que dixiese* ("How much better for me to have prided myself on what I might have written than to be shamed by what I have actually said"), he is using *expolitio*, subdivision *aferre contrarium*. And another of his favorite formulae, which consists of first denying the opposite of what he wishes to affirm ("not this but that") is *oppositio*, exemplified in a phrase at the end of the prologue: *porque reciba el pago no segund mi razón mas segund mi deseo* ("and so give me thanks not for what I have written, but for my desire to please you"). As for the two classes of ornament, *ornamentum facile* (easy ornament) alone would require a chapter to itself.[39]

Without, however, going into any technical detail, it is possible to say some more meaningful things about the style of San Pedro than that it is "rhetorical," "elegant," or "artificial." It is, first of all, logic adorned, a studied, self-conscious, and thoughtful style which aspires to beauty; the laments, letters, and speeches in particular are as carefully worked and polished as any piece of verse; there is simply not the remotest attempt to imitate colloquial speech. And in *Prison of Love* the ornamentation is matched to a dense content of thought; indeed much of the ornamentation derives from the balancing of thoughts, and it is hardly possible to separate "style" from "content"; how can one determine whether the syntax is governed by the syllogistic thought or whether the rhetorical devices used dictate a form of logical exposition? And finally, though San Pedro has given up using the tinsel of acoustic conceits, the prose of *Prison of Love* is a sonorous, subtly rhythmic prose, which betrays a poet's ear. It would require a book to itself for an adequate analysis.

VII *The Perfect Courtly Romance*

It is easy to see that in *Prison of Love* San Pedro has in a number of ways improved on his earlier attempt to write a "sentimental novel" or "courtly romance." He has raised the social

level of the setting; his hero is a perfect courtier and irreproachable lover, the constancy and perfection of whose love is demonstrated by his martyrdom; his heroine is a perfect lady, com-
pounded of compassion and concern for her honor; he
has contrived to cast over the whole work an air of archetypal
simplicity; the story is not marred by irrelevant or discordant
digression; the plotting is in general tauter, more complex, and
more plausible; an extraordinary variety of *praeexercitamenta*
(the set pieces) contribute to an extraordinarily unified whole;
and the style is subtle, solemn, and rich. San Pedro has achieved
a kind of perfection.

But perfection cannot be achieved without some sacrifice, and
we have also lost something. The idealization of the characters
and the dreamlike unreality of the setting leave no room for the
irrelevant but picturesque human detail which enlivens a work
like *Celestina*; there is not one touch of humor, and the tale of
the passion of Leriano is wrapped in the same atmosphere of
gloom, agony, despair, and death which could be held to be
a fault of *The Versified Passion*; the work is ardently profeminist
and invests the cult of love with the dignity of a religion, but
the romance lacks someone like Belisa, who in some measure
shows what comfort may be derived from "the endearing ele-
gance of female friendship" (as Dr. Johnson put it); and the
imperfect and unpredictable Arnalte is somehow more interesting
even in his selfishness and absurdities than the departicularized
Leriano.

The underlying assumption of all medieval thought, that there
was, theoretically, a perfect way of doing everything, produced
its formal triumphs, but also its nonsense. The manuals which
gave instruction on every aspect of life became ever more rigid
and complex—dictating the correct way to break up and carry
home a stag after a kill, or how many shelves for displaying
gold plate might be permitted in the chamber of a woman in
childbirth.[40] And San Pedro, discarding the impurities which
had entered his earlier effort, produced a courtly romance which
is the logical conclusion of certain trends and assumptions, but
which, having achieved this perfection, demonstrates that there
was, perhaps, something wrong with the premises.

Prison of Love represents perfection of its own kind; and it achieved a European success. But the fact that *Arnalte and Lucenda* was almost equally popular in France and Italy, and more popular in England, argues that the defects of the earlier romance were not manifest to a majority of ordinary readers. *Prison of Love* is the supreme example of the courtly romance, but the extremist San Pedro had reached the end of a line. His book was enormously influential in a great many different ways: in starting a vogue for "sentimental novels" in Italy, France, England, and Germany, in the conception of the perfect courtier,[41] in the losing battle which the feminists waged against the antifeminists,[42] in some of the ways it conceived of love, in the development of the epistolary novel, in its style of balanced periods (which could be imitated in translation), and so on. But it had no true successor.

CHAPTER 8

Minor Verse

I *The Panegyric on Isabella*

IN *Arnalte and Lucenda*, Arnalte, to reassure himself (as we later discover) that the Author is a man he can confide in, asks him about the Queen of Spain, and the Author answers him in verse with 210 lines of eulogy.[1] The poem can be dated about 1480 or 1481, between the end of the War of Succession and the opening of the campaign against Granada, because of the poet's repeated references to the peace now enjoyed by Castile and his failure to refer to Isabella as the moving spirit of a new Crusade against Islam. The Téllez-Girón twins abandoned their resistance to Isabella in 1476, but refused to aid her against their former friends and allies; and although their later wholehearted devotion to her cause gained them her confidence, she must still have felt in 1480 and 1481 that the Giróns were among her potential enemies. San Pedro at that period was already in the service of the Count of Urueña, and it is highly probable that his extremely flattering poem was written primarily to indicate to Isabella that she could in future count on the loyalty of the erstwhile rebel.[2]

The political background explains two of the oddities about the poem; one, its largely irrelevant presence in a courtly romance, and, two, the fact that San Pedro neither asks for any favor nor thanks the Queen for any favor received. There are a very large number of almost completely unstudied laudatory poems addressed to living people, from the twelfth- and thirteenth-century verses addressed to monarchs, to the fifteenth-century poems addressed by writers to their patrons, and those in which the poem is not prompted by the wish to acknowledge a favor shown or to ask for one are rare indeed.[3]

There is a further oddity about the poem, and that is that

while the panegyric, *laus* or *enkomion,* was a clearly defined genre in the medieval manuals of rhetoric,[4] San Pedro for once shows himself to be either unacquainted with or careless of the rules. He ignores, for instance, the obligatory introduction which speaks of the subject's glorious ancestry; he mixes up the sections praising the Queen's virtues with the section praising her beauty; he does not list her virtues in the recommended order; and only the last part, which was to speak of the probable judgment of posterity and the subject's reception in Paradise, shows that San Pedro knew of some manual or model. A consequence of not following the rules is that the poem is somewhat shapeless: the units are the individual stanzas, but they are set one after the other in a strangely incoherent way, most untypical of our author.

As for the content, since the object of the exercise is to praise Isabella, we find nothing but superlative phrases of adulation. Nothing else was permissible. But while we may read with a certain skepticism the fulsome praises of her beauty, the rest is by no means a list of clichés, but a rather specific listing of the things which the young Queen had already accomplished by 1480. This is done, of course, in general terms: San Pedro does not refer to the Cortes of Madrigal of 1476 or the Cortes of Toledo of 1480, but he does say (and it is scarcely a commonplace of panegyric) that she cut short unnecessary delay (*es atajo de entrevalos*) and this was certainly one of her most important judicial reforms. Anyone who knows the early accomplishments of Isabella can easily attach specific instances to every phrase which San Pedro uses. It is not, in short, completely empty flattery, but shows that the poet, and no doubt the Count of Urueña, truly appreciated the political sagacity of Isabella's moves.

It is interesting, too, to see the way in which San Pedro dressed up his material with all the rhetorical tricks at his command. Some devices are taken to unacceptable extremes, such as the piece of *repetitio* in which sixteen consecutive lines begin with *es*; some examples of *comparatio* are distinctly far-fetched; and the devices of *annominatio* and *traductio* produce a stanza like the following (which I make no attempt to translate):

Nunca haze descon*cierto,*
en todo y por todo a*cierta,*
sigue a Dios, que es lo más *cierto,*
y descon*cierta* el con*cierto*
que lo contrario con*cierta.*

(The second *quintilla* of this stanza repeats "re*quiere,*" "*quiere,*" "*quiera,*" "*quiere,*" and "*quiere.*")

The significance of the panegyric in the poetic trajectory of San Pedro is its striking contrast with the religious poetry, *The Passion* and *The Seven Sorrows,* which latter poem could well have been written about the same time. Instead of the plain style demanded for the exposition of religious topics, he has adopted the elevated style required for "elevated" subjects. He rejects the easy rhyme of *similiter cadens* (verb endings, etc.) for the difficult rhyme of *similiter desinens* (*maravilla-manzilla-Castilla; modo-lodo-todo;* etc.). It demonstrates once more, so marked is the contrast between the two long poems inserted in *Arnalte and Lucenda,* that we can hardly talk of "San Pedro's style," for he was a writer of such extreme versatility that he could employ whatever style seemed to him best to suit his purpose.

II *The Short Love Poems*

It is to be presumed that San Pedro's minor pieces—none of which can be precisely dated—were written over a span of time which must have embraced both *Arnalte and Lucenda* and *Prison of Love.* None appeared in print before the *Cancionero general* of 1511, but since they are all love poems, of the kind he was to condemn in his *Desprecio de la Fortuna* (*Contempt of Fortune*), we can safely place them in the period during which San Pedro wrote for the amusement of the ladies of the Queen and the young nobles of the court. They can be dated, that is, approximately between 1480 and 1492.

At first glance, since they are all relatively short, are in octosyllables, treat of love, and employ a restricted vocabulary, it is their sameness which strikes the reader; and they are, of course, instantly identifiable as belonging to that variety of Spanish poetry which is called, usually contemptuously, "*cancionero*

verse." But there is considerable variety within this superficial uni-
formity. Although San Pedro invariably employs the octosyllabic
line in all his verse, he uses in his shorter poems a wide variety
of strophic forms, and his repertoire includes *canciones, esparsas,
romances* (with rhyme instead of the assonance usually associated
with this form), and *villancicos*. In length they range from the
brief three lines of the *invenciones* to be found in *Arnalte and
Lucenda* up to a stanzaic piece of 120 lines. All make use of some
rhetorical device or ornament, but they also exhibit a diversity
of style, from the relatively simple syntax and vocabulary of
the *romances* and *villancicos* (roughly approximate to the ballads and the popular lyrics of medieval England) to the almost
indecipherable complexity of a *canción* which was to be praised
by the seventeenth-century authority Gracián as the most
extraordinary example of paradox and concentrated wit that
he knew of.[5]

Several are occasional poems, prompted by real or imaginary
incidents, such as "Dama tan poco constante" ("Oh, Inconstant
Lady"), written (as the rubric explains) because he gave her
a love letter concealed in a glove, and she shamelessly showed
it to some young nobles who were also courting her, so that they
could make fun of him; "El hilo qu'en este día" ("The Piece of
Cloth[6] Which You Today . . .") gracefully acknowledges the gift
of a piece of linen; "No temo, dama real" ("Oh Royal Lady,
I Have No Fear") answers his mistress who had told him he
must not curse himself or he would go to Hell; and the grotesque
"Más hermosa que cortés" ("More Beautiful Than Lady-like")
returns a shattering answer to the lady of whom he begged a
kiss, and who replied with an obscenity. He composes poems on
special days such as Palm Sunday, Easter Monday, Low Sunday, ingeniously improvising some delicate compliment to his
mistress based on the day and its significance. An extraordinary
ingenuity and fertility of invention are frequently apparent,
whether the occasion suggests the opportunity to him, or whether
he stage-manages his own occasion, writing a little verse for a
gypsy-woman to go and recite to his lady. Both his *romances*
cleverly parody older traditional ballads.

Cancionero verse in general has suffered from neglect and
uninformed scorn since the end of the nineteenth century and

is only now beginning to be understood and appreciated. The reasons for its general condemnation by the critics are, partly, that there is a great deal of it and that much, since an amazing number of courtiers did try their hand at writing verse, is of indifferent quality; partly, that much still remains inaccessible or inadequately edited; partly, that some of it is not intelligible without an informed commentary from an editor familiar with its very special vocabulary (the casual reader can too often either not understand it at all or think he has understood it, when the point of what he has taken for a vapid and vacuous poem lies in a series of double meanings); and partly, that nineteenth- and, unfortunately, some twentieth-century critics inherited from the Romantics unjustifiable notions of what poetry *ought* to be.

Cancionero verse must be judged by its own values. So far as the poets of the latter part of the fifteenth century are concerned, it is clear that, at least in their nonreligious, nonmoral, nonpolitical amorous verse, we are entitled to look for wit, brevity, originality, ingenuity, and verbal and rhetorical felicity, and in fact there are very few poems in which one does not find some clear attempt to be ingeniously original or to find a felicitous phrasing for an old idea. The "tired clichés" (*cansados clisés*), which historians of Spanish literature seem to think the hallmark of this kind of verse, are rarely to be found, even among the least talented of the aristocratic dilettantes. Menéndez Pelayo and those who have subscribed to his judgments seem to have mistaken for a series of clichés poems which do restrict themselves to a very special and limited vocabulary, so that certain words like *vida, muerte, gloria, dolor, razón,* etc., occur with high frequency;[7] and there are some conceits and paradoxes which recur rather insistently. But many of these ideas—such as that love is joy and pain, or that the lover longs to reveal his secret and must keep silent—are simply the received ideas of the time, which no poet makes a *special* point of expressing: these more obvious paradoxical conceits are not, in fact, the real point of the poems which contain them, and the wit and ingenuity to be found lie elsewhere, if in no more than the novelty of the phraseology. As for the vocabulary, its deliberate reduction to a comparative handful of abstract terms results in the creation of ambiguities which are exploited, sometimes rather naughtily, by a series of poets.

Because of the very special language in which they are written, it is virtually impossible to translate many of these poems, and a brief example may serve to show why this is so. In San Pedro's "El mayor bien de quereros" ("The Greatest Benefit I Receive from Loving You"), the three lines immediately following the first two are each susceptible of alternative interpretations, depending on what meaning we attach to the verbs *perder* and *perderse* (for which the Dictionary of the Real Academia Española lists a total of twenty-five different senses); and San Pedro (much more subtly than in many a coarse medieval riddle or than in Sir John Suckling's "Candle" riddle)[8] deliberately misdirects the reader by appearing to suggest that he is reflecting on the desirability of putting an end to his painful desire by consummating it, perhaps by force (*perderos* would then mean "ruin you," in a euphemistic sexual sense), and the reader is carried along, satisfied with this sense of the statement and its consequent explanation (satisfied with the sense, that is, if not the sentiment), until he is brought up short by a further explanation which makes nonsense of the first, and he is sent back to try another meaning of *perder* until he discovers that *perderos* can mean no more than "to forget you," and everything falls into place.

This extremely summary analysis was not calculated to engender enthusiasm for *cancionero* verse. I suspect, indeed, that for its contemporary audience, the pleasure to be derived from some of these poems was not dissimilar from the intellectual satisfaction gained from solving a crossword puzzle; and that is no fun if someone else does it for you. I intended to show the difficulty of interpreting such poetry to non-Hispanists, to emphasize that it is demonstrable that critics and even editors have not understood some of this verse, and to indicate that the values of this verse are quite different from those of most of the verse we are accustomed to. No one would contend that there are not serious obstacles in the way of its proper understanding and appreciation, but they are obstacles created by its subtlety, ingenuity, abstraction, and intellectualism—and possibly its lack of really serious import. The poetry often seems flirtatious rather than genuinely passionate; it is frequently the poetry of the *game* of love rather than of love, Ovidian rather than solemn or tragic. But we are only just beginning to build the bridge from ourselves to it.

In his short poems, Diego de San Pedro demonstrates once again what a superb craftsman he was. And it also reveals him again reacting to his environment, producing the poem for the occasion, amusing the nobles of the court, and, in two poems at least, yet once again taking matters to a superlative extreme: in "Más hermosa que cortés" outdoing his contemporaries in obscenity, and in "El mayor bien de quereros" creating perhaps the most difficult poem in the *Cancionero general,* which Gracián (possibly the last critic to understand it) was to praise in superlative terms.

CHAPTER 9

Desprecio de la Fortuna
(Contempt of Fortune)

I *Fortune*

THE arbitrary and inexplicable disasters which have beset human beings from time immemorial have from the beginning of historical time, and no doubt before, preoccupied the thought of men. "Chance" and "destiny" were more than once rationally explained, but the atavistic superstitions which made capricious supernatural beings the cause of the vicissitudes of human life were never extinguished.[1] It was, however, only toward the end of the classical period in Rome that the ancient Italian Fors Fortuna, goddess of fertility, became that omnipotent deity, Fortune, who was to obsess the mind of medieval man. *Constans in levitate sua* ("constant only in her inconstancy"), as Ovid said,[2] she governed all worldly wealth and honor, but could not touch virtue: *Nihil eripit Fortuna, nisi quod dedit: virtutem autem non dat,* said Seneca ("Fortune can take away only what she bestowed: and virtue is not in her gift").[3]

Christianity did not put an end to the belief in Fortune; there were some Christian apologists, from St. Augustine[4] to St. Thomas Aquinas,[5] who denied the existence of any supernatural power which might be called "Fortune," but others, like St. Jerome,[6] chose to equate Fortune with one of the Devil's ministers. And in hundreds of medieval authors it is really quite impossible to tell whether "Fortune" is merely an allegory of chance, a useful metaphor, whether she is a malignant accomplice of Satan, or the humble handmaiden of Providence, as in Dante[7] (a very rare exception among profane authors).

One of the greatest and most influential books in the history of Western literature is Boethius's *De consolatione Philosophiae* (*On the Consolation of Philosophy*). The *Consolation* enjoyed

126

the most remarkable diffusion, and we find medieval translations
in Anglo-Saxon (King Alfred's), English (two), German (two),
French (more than four), Greek, Dutch, Provençal, Italian,
Catalan, and Castilian.[8] But Boethius's book was perhaps just
a shade too subtly presented for the medieval mind, for when
Philosophy first appears to Boethius in his cell—disgraced, under-
going torture, and awaiting execution—she begins by speaking
of "Fortune" as though that arbitrary goddess did really exist,
and it is only gradually that she weans Boethius from his despair
and self-pity, brings him to the realization that "Fortune" is a
myth, and, in the difficult fourth and fifth books, reveals to
him the grand design of the cosmos. "Fortune" vanishes, and
the inexplicable confusion, anarchy, mortality, decay, and agi-
tation of human life are shown to be insignificant. Most medieval
writers, even those most patently and obviously influenced by
Boethius, seem to have fixed on the early books (where Philosophy maintains the fiction of the existence of Fortune) and to
have forgotten, rejected, or simply failed to understand the
message of the last two books. Boccaccio's influential *De casibus
virorum et feminarum illustrium* (*On the Fall of Great Men
and Women*) is little more than a catalogue of notorious disasters occasioned by Fortune (Alexander the Great, Julius Caesar,
Darius, Pompey, etc., etc.), while Petrarch's *De remediis
utriusque Fortunae* (*On Defending Oneself against Fortune,
Good or Bad*) offers only the Stoic remedy of detachment.

In the Spanish fifteenth century, lists of the fallen are provided by, among others, Gonzalo Martínez de Medina, Juan de
Mena, and the Marquis of Santillana, while the Marquis proffers
Stoic remedies in his *Bías contra Fortuna* (*Bias* [a proper name]
against Fortune). Only a handful of profane writers appear to
have comprehended the incompatibility of Christianity with the
notion of Fortune, and none endeavored to explain at length that
no hay más Fortuna que Dios ("there is no such thing as Fortune; there is only God").

II Contempt of Fortune

We have seen (Chapter 1) that at the conclusion of the
Granada campaign Don Juan Téllez-Girón retired to his estates

in Andalusia, and to the company of his exceedingly devout wife, to devote himself to good works, and that Diego de San Pedro, beginning to feel that he was growing old, probably accompanied his master in his self-imposed exile from the court. The ever adaptable San Pedro, urged to break a long silence, found a new theme. It is quite clear that he had been reading both Boethius and some of the so-called Ambrosian dialogues of Seneca, certainly *De vita beata* (*On the Happy Life*) and possibly *De tranquillitate animi* (*On Peace of Mind*) and *De providentia* (*On Providence*).[9] And in Genesis, Job, and the prophetic books of the Bible like Isaiah and Jeremiah, he found matter to support what he now wanted to say. His theme was appropriate for the man the Count had become, and San Pedro, isolated and alone, conscious of his grey hair, and living (if we can believe him) in straitened circumstances, was beginning to think of the imminence of death and the possibility that he had misspent his talents.

The poet starts by disowning all his early erotic works (although one senses a certain ambivalence, a certain pride, in the way he so carefully lists and describes each one) and then, invoking God's aid, embarks on his theme. For a thousand years Boethius had not been fully understood, and it would be rash to say that San Pedro was the first to recover the Boethian message—for one thing, since his *Contempt of Fortune* is a much shorter work, of only 410 lines, he is obliged to discard a great deal of Boethian material. He comes to no blinding Neoplatonic climax; he keeps returning to the theme of the miseries of this world; and he seems pessimistically to dwell on death as an ending rather than as a gateway to another life. But at the same time he spares us the medieval catalogue of the victims of Fortune, a full list of possible disasters, the complicated medieval allegory of the Wheel of Fortune, and even fails to play with the "constancy" of Fortune's "inconstancy"; and he included so much genuine Boethius that we have a work which comes closer to Boethius than anything but some translations of the *Consolation.*

Our reason is free, and only to understand the nature of good and bad fortune is to free oneself from the tyranny of fear; poverty and death are not enemies but allies, aiding us to live virtuously; riches and fame (though fame is the last ambition a noble soul abandons) are of singularly little importance; contentment lies in being satisfied with our lot; man's unhappiness comes from sin, from Avarice, Envy, Lust, Vainglory, and Pride; the whole world is mad, but the poet, at the end of his life, has now seen the light of reason, and neither fears nor desires anything more. It is a remarkably sober, dignified, and moving statement, and time and again San Pedro produces a superb, simple, memorable, extremely effective stanza which challenges comparison with the best of Jorge Manrique's stanzas written on the death of his father. For once, however, San Pedro's success took a different form: what he sparked off was a new appetite for the genuine Boethius; he did not start, but put an end to the series of poems about Fortune; and his *Contempt of Fortune* has been totally neglected by the critics.[10]

CHAPTER 10

Conclusion

MEDIEVAL and Renaissance writers were rarely specialists producing only verse or only prose, only short stories or letters or sermons or epics or plays or novels or treatises, for there was no reason why a writer properly trained in rhetorical technique could not turn his hand to any literary form; but the versatility of Diego de San Pedro is noteworthy even in the fifteenth century, not only for the variety of forms and topics which he was prepared to tackle, but for the chameleon-like way in which he adapted his style and language to the matter in hand or the audience to which it was to be addressed.

Numerous little phrases throughout his works[1] show that he was ever ready to produce what was demanded of him and that he was consumed by an anxiety to please and to ingratiate himself with his superiors. It is a trait of his personality which could lead us to despise him, were we not forced to admire his superb professionalism, the versatility of his talent, and the certainty of his judgment. The directives he was given were vague enough: his nun (if she asked at all) wanted him to tell the story of the Passion of Christ in Spanish; some ladies desired to hear him preach; the Alcaide de los Donceles wanted him to write another love story; some gentlemen said that they thought it was a pity he seemed to have given up writing. San Pedro was forced to guess at what precisely would please most.

Because of his extraordinary sensitivity to the contemporary atmosphere and because of his knowledge of Latin,[2] he was able to pick out of the air half-formed ideas and attitudes and clothe them in words to produce what can only be described as a series of best sellers. We have seen how he exploited the *Meditationes vitae Christi* to respond to new currents of religious thought, and with what acuity he retained and discarded earlier material,

130

so that, of all the versified Passions or lives of Christ, his alone was still a popular work into the latter half of the nineteenth century. We have seen how he initiated poems on the Seven Sorrows of Mary; how he created the Ovidian tale in Spanish and achieved a European success with *Arnalte and Lucenda;* how he formulated a code of love and showed it in action in *Prison of Love,* another resounding success; how close he got to creating the epistolary novel; how perceptive he was in giving the Count of Urueña almost unadulterated Boethius; how he changed his prose style and became a rhetorical model for Europe. It is an amazing record of success. And we have seen too how much, good and bad, was due to a peculiar extremist streak in his personality, manifested in a consistent tendency to push something to its logical conclusion, to be, if not the first, then the "most," as with "El mayor bien de quereros" or "Más hermosa que cortés."

The literature of fifteenth-century Spain has long been over-shadowed by the achievements of the writers of the Golden Age; but the fifteenth century is gradually coming into its own. The historians have already recognized that the seeds of the greatness of Imperial Spain, as well as its subsequent decline and collapse, are again and again to be traced back to the events of the Isabelline period, and the institutions and modes of thought established then; but the traditionalist historians of literature prefer to date Spain's Golden Age from the Italianizing innovations of Boscán and Garcilaso. While it is well known that many of the works which were most widely read in the sixteenth century were products of the fifteenth century—Mena's *Labyrinth,* Jorge Manrique's elegy on the death of his father, *Prison of Love, Celestina, Amadis of Gaul*—it is less fully appreciated that they were the indispensable basis for much of what came after. We may eventually come to recognize that the literature of the Golden Age rests on Isabelline foundations. It may then be possible more justly to assess how very different Spanish literature might have been without the contribution of Diego de San Pedro.

Notes and References

Chapter One

1. Marcelino Menéndez y Pelayo, *Orígenes de la novela,* 4 vols., *NBAE,* I, VII, XIV, and XXI (Madrid: Bailly-Baillière, 1905–1915); Edición Nacional (Santander: C. S. I. C., 1962), II, 31. The documents he cites were discovered by Francisco Rodríguez Marín and Manuel Serrano y Sanz.

2. Nicolás Antonio, *Bibliotheca hispana vetus,* II (Rome: Antonio de Rubeis, 1696), No. 326; in the revised ed. by Pérez Bayer (Madrid: Joaquín Ibarra, 1783–1788), the entry appears on p. 249. There is a facsimile reprint of the latter edition (Turin: Bottega d'Erasmo, 1963). For further details, see my "Two San Pedros," *Bulletin of Hispanic Studies,* XLII (1965), 255–58, and the introduction to Vol. I of my edition of the *Obras completas* of San Pedro (Madrid: Castalia, 1973).

3. The information about this Diego de San Pedro appears on f. 20r. Pellicer quotes the two stanzas which refer to the five noble Castilian houses of greatest antiquity, Haro, Lara, Villamayor, Guzmán, and Castro. The same verses are cited also by Luis Bartolomé de Salazar y Castro in his *Historia genealógica de la Casa de Lara,* 4 vols. (Madrid: M. de Llanos y Guzmán, 1694–1697), I, 24.

4. The will in which Don Pedro left 20,000 *maravedises* to the *bachiller* Diego de San Pedro is extant in the Archivo de la Casa de Osuna, *bolsa* 19, no. 1, and was published by Francisco R. de Uhagón as an appendix to the lecture he gave on his admission to the Real Academia de la Historia, *Las órdenes militares* (Madrid: Real Academia de la Historia, 1898). Other documents in those archives, used by Menéndez Pelayo, are *bolsa* 9, Y, *legajo* 1, nos. 14, 15, and 16, and *bolsa* 10, *legajo* 1, nos. 5 and 6. Other references, including the epitaph, are to be found in the investigation of the lineage of Don Alonso de Fonseca conducted by the *Junta de las Órdenes* (Council of the Military Orders) in 1592 (Archivo Histórico Nacional, Santiago 3120).

5. For the texts, see my edition of the *Obras completas* of San Pedro: II, *Cárcel de Amor* (Madrid: Castalia, 1972), and III, *Poesías* (*ibidem,* forthcoming). They can also be read in the edition by

133

Samuel Gili Gaya of San Pedro's (incomplete) *Obras,* Clásicos Castellanos 133 (Madrid: Espasa-Calpe, 1950; 1958; 1967).

6. The list, dated November 14, 1467, appears on folios 15v–31r of the Archivo Histórico Nacional (AHN), Santiago 3120.

7. Ángel Valbuena Prat, *Historia de la literatura española,* 3 vols., 3rd ed. (Barcelona: Gustavo Gili, 1950), I, 281, alleges that the title page of his most important work (i.e., *Cárcel de Amor* [*Prison of Love*]) describes him as castellan of Peñafiel; in fact, only one edition gives him the titles of *bachiller* and *alcaide* and that is the modern edition by Jorge Rubió y Balaguer (Barcelona: Gustavo Gili, 1941), who took the information from Menéndez Pelayo.

8. *Ed. cit.,* p. 170.

9. For detailed discussion of the chronology and dating of San Pedro's works, see Vol. I of my edition of the *Obras completas;* I avoid these technicalities in the present volume.

10. Luis Zapata, *Miscelánea,* ed. Pascual Gayangos, Memorial Histórico Español XI (Madrid: Real Academia de la Historia, 1859), 395. See Menéndez Pelayo, *Orígenes, ed. cit.,* III, 60.

11. For a list of other versified Passions see Antonio Pérez Gómez, "La pasión trobada de Diego de San Pedro," *Revista de Literatura,* I (1952), 163–82.

12. Eugenio Asensio, *Itinerario del entremés* (Madrid: Gredos, 1965), p. 160.

13. Emilio Cotarelo y Mori, "Nuevos y curiosos datos biográficos del famoso trovador y novelista Diego de San Pedro," *Boletín de la Real Academia Española,* XIV (1927), 305–26. The documents in question are inquiries made as the result of applications to enter one or other of the Military Orders of Alcántara and Santiago by Don Antonio de Fonseca in 1569 (AHN, Alcántara 550), Don Alonso de Fonseca in 1592 (AHN, Santiago 3120), and Don Pedro de Fonseca in 1599 (AHN, Alcántara 551). The applicants had to be not only noble (mere proofs of nobility are concerned only with the paternal line of descent) but also free of all taint or suspicion of Jewish blood.

14. I have attempted to show how Cotarelo misread and misinterpreted this evidence in "Was Diego de San Pedro a *converso?* A Re-examination of Cotarelo's Documentary Evidence," *Bulletin of Hispanic Studies,* XXXIV (1957), 187–200.

15. Miguel Lasso de la Vega y López de Tejada, Marqués del Saltillo, *Discurso leído en la Universidad de Oviedo, con motivo de la solemne apertura del curso de 1929 a 1930: La embajada en Alemania del conde de Oñate y la elección de Fernando II rey de romanos (1616–1620)* (Madrid: Tipografía de Alberto Fontana, 1929). Ap-

pendix II cites passages from the investigation into the lineage of Don Íñigo Vélez de Guevara, fifth Count of Oñate (AHN, Santiago 3671), who was related to the Fonsecas.

16. See Julio Atienza, *Nobiliario español: Diccionario heráldico de apellidos españoles y de títulos nobiliarios*, 3rd revised and enlarged ed. (Madrid: Aguilar, 1959), *s.v.* "San Pedro."

17. Stephen Gilman, in *The Spain of Fernando de Rojas* (Princeton: Princeton University Press, 1972), relies on a further argument to sustain the thesis of San Pedro's Jewish origins: alleging (without a shred of supporting evidence) that he was the *mayordomo* of "Don Pedro Téllez Girón" (a linguistic cross, one presumes, of Pedro Girón and Juan Téllez-Girón), he goes on to assert that the office of *mayordomo* was peculiarly a prerogative of *conversos*, and hence that San Pedro must have been of Jewish stock (see especially pp. 263 and 327). Others, including Julio Caro Baroja, *Vidas mágicas e Inquisición* (Madrid: Taurus, 1967), I, 284, have detected his *converso* origins in the "bitter humor" and "restrained irony" of *Prison of Love*. What humor? What irony?

18. Francisco Márquez Villanueva, " 'Cárcel de amor,' novela política," *Revista de Occidente*, 2nd series, XIV (1966), 185–200.

19. References to these two magnates may be found in all the contemporary chronicles and modern histories of the period. Jorge Manrique, in his *Coplas por la muerte de su padre*, referred to them as "those two brothers, the Grand Masters, as rich and powerful as kings, whom high and low were obliged to obey" (*los otros dos hermanos, / Maestres tan prosperados / como reyes, / a los grandes y medianos / trajeron tan sojuzgados / a sus leyes*).

20. The fullest history of the Girón family, which draws on an astonishingly wide variety of sources (see Vol. I of my ed. of the *Obras completas*, 13), is Dr. Gerónimo Gudiel's *Compendio de algunas historias de España, donde se tratan muchas antigüedades dignas de memoria: y especialmente se da noticia de la antigua familia de los Girones y de otros muchos linajes* (Alcalá: Juan Íñiguez de Lequerica, 1577). Gudiel, f. 97v, follows Diego Enríquez del Castillo, *Crónica del rey don Enrique IV* (repr. in BAE, LXX), in noting that for twenty-four hours Isabella prayed to God "to carry off one of them sooner than permit the marriage to take place" (*antes llevasse a uno dellos que el matrimonio se effectuasse*), and adds "the death of so powerful a baron was, it seems, inevitable, when such a woman pleaded with God for it to happen" (*muerte de tan poderoso varón, parece avía de suceder, rogado y suplicado nuestro Señor por tal muger*). Her lady, Doña Beatriz de Bobadilla, in fact is reported to have offered to murder Don Pedro for her.

21. Gudiel, f. 98v, explains that her father "gave" her to Don Pedro on the understanding that he would seek Papal dispensation to marry her.

22. There is a good deal of confusion between Urueña and Ureña. Both places (Ureña is now a *despoblado*, a deserted ruin, in the province of Salamanca) belonged to the Giróns, and in the sixteenth century (in the ballads for instance) "Ureña" seems to become the preferred form. Nevertheless, the original title was "of Urueña."

23. See F. Fernández de Bethencourt, *Historia genealógica y heráldica de la monarquía española*, 9 vols. (Madrid: E. Teodoro, 1897–1912), II, 528–33.

24. The date is given incorrectly as 1477 by Gerónimo Zurita, *Anales de la Corona de Aragón*, 7 vols. (Zaragoza: Pedro Bernus, 1562–1579), Book XX, Chapter II, and consequently by Samuel Gili Gaya in the introduction to his edition of the *Obras* of San Pedro, p. XXVIII. There is a modern reprint of Zurita, ed. Angel Canellas López (Zaragoza: Institución Fernando el Católico, 1970–   ).

25. See Fernández de Bethencourt, *op. cit.*, VI, 102. Bernardino died shortly afterwards and Catalina in 1476 married Don Alfonso Fernández de Córdoba de Aguilar, "el Grande," an uncle of the Alcaide de los Donceles to whom San Pedro dedicated *Prison of Love*.

26. See Agustín Durán, *Romancero general*, 2 vols., BAE, X and XVI (1849 and 1851), Nos. 1095–99, 1101–5, and 1108–12.

27. See Fernández de Bethencourt, *op. cit.*, IX, 39–53.

28. At the very least these included (in 1483) Mora, Montefrío, Loja, and the battle of Alhama; (in 1485) Coín, Ronda, and Marbella; (in 1487) Vélez-Málaga and Málaga; and (in 1489) Baza.

29. She is wrongly identified by Cotarelo, *art. cit.*, and consequently by Gili Gaya, *ed. cit.*, as a certain Doña María Manuel, who was in fact not born until after 1510. See my "The Mysterious Marina Manuel (Prologue, *Cárcel de Amor*)," *Studia Iberica: Festschrift für Hans Flasche* (Berne: Francke Verlag, 1973), pp. 689–95, or, for briefer details, my introduction to Vol. I of San Pedro's *Obras completas*, where I also publish her portrait.

30. *Cárcel de Amor, ed. cit.*, p. 80.

31. For evidence and references, see "The Mysterious Marina Manuel," *cit. supra*, note 29.

32. Among the rhyming relations of Don Juan Téllez-Girón, who has himself two compositions in the *Cancionero general* (the second being added in 1514), one might cite his twin brother Rodrigo, his cousin the Marquis of Villena, his father-in-law the Constable of Castile, and his son-in-law the Duke of Medina Sidonia.

33. Cartagena was killed at the second siege of Loja in 1486.

The poem can be found in the *Cancionero general* (Valencia, 1511), facsimile with introduction by Antonio Rodríguez-Moñino (Madrid: Real Academia Española, 1958), f. 143v. Doña Marina was also the recipient of a long love poem addressed to her by Diego López de Haro, *ibid.*, f. 65r–65v.

34. In addition to Dr. Gudiel and San Pedro himself, Fray Alberto de Aguayo, *Libro de Boecio Severino intitulado de la consolación de la philosophía* (Seville, 1518), facsimile by Antonio Pérez Gómez (Cieza: "la fonte que mana y corre," 1966), folios 2v–3v, speaks in striking terms of the Count's saintliness. Although Don Juan's largesse reduced his father's immense fortune, possibly by two-thirds, and his own financial status among the Spanish grandees perhaps to eleventh, his income still amounted to some 20,000 ducats a year shortly before his death. See Lucio Marineo Sículo, *Cosas memorables de España* (Alcalá de Henares: Juan de Brocar, 1539), folios 24–25. (Note that this is not even the first vernacular edition, and that the Spanish translation was preceded by various Latin editions.)

35. *Obras completas*, III.

36. Diego Hurtado de Mendoza, *Guerra de Granada* (Lisbon: G. de la Viña, 1627), ed. B. Blanco-González (Madrid: Castalia, 1970), notes, p. 103, that "the Count of Ureña escaped, though giving some occasion for scurrilous songs" (*dando ocasión a los cantares y libertad española*). Some ballads do indeed accuse him reproachfully: *Decid, conde de Ureña, / Don Alonso ¿dónde queda?*, etc. The truth seems to be that Don Alonso simply refused to retreat in an impossible situation.

37. In this case any censure must fall on Ferdinand, who, for readily comprehensible reasons, exceeded his legal authority. Whatever devious motives may have inspired Juan Manuel, Juan Téllez-Girón was assuredly not seeking personal advantage.

38. Andrea Navagiero, *Il viaggio fatto in Spagna et in Francia* (Venice: D. Farri, 1563), f. 17.

39. See Vol. I of my edition of the *Obras completas*. An article which I wrote in collaboration with J. S. Cummins (who discovered the documents in question), "An Approximate Date for the Death of Diego de San Pedro," *Bulletin of Hispanic Studies*, XXXVI (1959), 226–29, is invalidated because of the confusion of the *alcaide* with the author. We proved only that the *alcaide* was certainly dead by 1514; but the only reason for supposing he was alive at all in the interval between 1472 and 1514 was the literary activity of our author.

Chapter Two

1. Among innumerable readily available accounts, the opening

chapters of John H. Elliott, *Imperial Spain 1469–1716* (London: Arnold, 1963), can be specially recommended.

2. For the economic and social factors underlying these movements see Angus MacKay, "Popular Movements and Pogroms in Fifteenth-century Castile," *Past and Present*, No. 55 (May, 1972), 33–67. For the detailed and carefully documented history of just one city, undoubtedly far from untypical, see Eloy Benito Ruano, *Toledo en el siglo XV* (Madrid: C. S. I. C., 1961).

3. Just how far the history of the reign of Henry IV has been distorted by Isabelline chroniclers (in the same way as Tudor historians libeled Richard III) is something we are slowly discovering but about which we may never know the whole truth. Henry IV may have been less depraved than he has been painted; his folly and weakness can hardly have been exaggerated.

4. The point is well made by R. B. Tate in the introduction (in Spanish) to his edition of Fernán Pérez de Guzmán, *Generaciones y semblanzas* (London: Tamesis Books, 1965). See also his introduction (in English) to Fernando del Pulgar, *Claros varones de Castilla* (Oxford: Clarendon Press, 1971).

5. The most complete and up-to-date account is that contained in the two large volumes by Luis Suárez Hernández, Juan de Mata Carriazo, and Manuel Fernández Álvarez, *La España de los Reyes Católicos* (Madrid: Espasa-Calpe, 1969), *tomo* XVII of the *Historia de España* supervised by Ramón Menéndez Pidal. Still the fullest and most readable account in English, although inevitably inaccurate in certain details and particular points of emphasis, is William H. Prescott's *History of the Reign of Ferdinand and Isabella*, first published in 1837, but best read in the posthumous revised and enlarged version by John Foster Kirk (London: Sonnenschein, 1890).

6. Juan de Lucena, "Epístola exhortatoria a las letras," in *Opúsculos literarios de los siglos XIV a XVI*, ed. A. Paz y Melia (Madrid: Sociedad de Bibliófilos Españoles, 1892), p. 216.

7. See Fernando del Pulgar, *Crónica de los Reyes Católicos*, ed. Juan de Mata Carriazo, 2 vols. (Madrid: Espasa-Calpe, 1943), II, Chap. CC, 269.

8. It is worth noting also that, as Rafael Lapesa has shown, Spanish poets imitated the *content* of Italian and especially Petrarchan verse before they adopted its *forms*: see his "Poesía de cancioneros y poesía italianizante," first published in *Strenae: Estudios de filología e historia dedicados al Prof. Manuel García Blanco*, Acta Salmanticensia XVI (Salamanca: Facultad de Filosofía y Letras, 1962), and reprinted in his *De la Edad Media a nuestros días* (Madrid: Gredos, 1967), pp. 145–71.

9. "Otros cavalleros cortesanos": see the rubric-title of *Cárcel de Amor*, ed. *cit.*, p. 79.

10. He refers in this way to its success in the second stanza of his *Desprecio de la Fortuna*, ed. Gili Gaya, *loc. cit.*, p. 236; in *Obras completas, ed. cit.*, III.

Chapter Three

1. There can be no doubt about the direction in which this self-plagiarization took place: matter which fits perfectly the context of *The Passion* occasionally exhibits anomalous features in the context of *The Seven Sorrows*. See my "The Religious Poems of Diego de San Pedro: Their Relationship and Their Dating," *Hispanic Review*, XXVIII (1960), 1–15.

2. See Dorothy S. Severin, "The Earliest Version of Diego de San Pedro's 'La Pasión Trobada,'" *Romanische Forschungen*, LXXXI (1969), 176–92, and her introduction to *La Passión trobada: edición paleográfica . . . según la versión manuscrita del Cancionero de Oñate-Castañeda* (Naples: Istituto Universitario Orientale di Napoli, 1974).

3. In *The Passion*, for instance, San Pedro relies heavily on the "easy" rhymes offered by the Spanish conjugations: imperfects in *-aba* or *-ía*, past participles in *-ado* or *-ido*, etc., while in his *Contempt of Fortune* he usually eschews such facile solutions and prefers "difficult" rhymes like *canas-vanas-livianas, tal-mal-mortal*, etc.

4. For a full discussion of the bibliographical and textual problems involved, see my introduction to Vol. III of his *Obras completas* (an introduction which in this respect draws heavily on the work of Dorothy Severin—see note 2).

5. The reasons for discarding alternative hypotheses, such as that the additional stanzas were added *later*, perhaps by another hand, are set out in the introduction to Vol. III of the *Obras completas*.

6. For bibliography and further detail, see my "The Supposed Sources of Inspiration of Spanish Fifteenth-century Narrative Religious Verse," *Symposium*, Winter 1963, pp. 268–91. Much has been made of the alleged influence of the *Devotio moderna* (see note 25); there is no evidence that its essential texts were known in Spain before the 1490's, and the features I have mentioned are all characteristic of mendicant, and especially Franciscan, teaching.

7. I examined the sources of his exegesis of the episode of the Circumcision in the article cited in note 6. On Fray Íñigo's work we now have a series of excellent studies by Julio Rodriguez-Puértolas: his edition of the complete *Cancionero* (Madrid: Espasa-Calpe, 1968), his *Fray Íñigo de Mendoza y sus "Coplas de Vita Christi"* (Madrid: Gredos, 1968), and his "Estudios sobre Fray Íñigo de Mendoza," Part I

of his *De la Edad Media a la edad conflictiva* (Madrid: Gredos, 1972).

8. Both volumes were printed in the mid-1480's. See the most useful introduction by Sir Henry Thomas to his facsimile edition of the *Coplas* (London: British Museum, 1936).

9. This is a strangely neglected volume: almost everyone who mentions him (including Simón Díaz) refers only to the revised and enlarged edition of Toledo, 1508. A facsimile of the original volume was prepared by Sir Henry Thomas in the same year as the Román volume (London: British Museum, 1936).

10. For a complete analysis of the parts of the Gospels utilized and how San Pedro synthesized the four different versions of the Passion, see Dorothy Sherman Vivian (later Severin), " 'La Passión trobada' de Diego de San Pedro y sus relaciones con el drama medieval de la Pasión," *Anuario de Estudios Medievales*, I (1964), 451–70, where they are set out in the long note 23, pp. 458–59. They are also indicated *seriatim* in Vol. III of the *Obras completas*.

11. It appears in the *Legenda aurea* (*Golden Legend*) of Jacob of Voragine, in Chap. XLV, "De sancto Mathia apostolo" (since Mathias replaced Judas to make up the twelve). The best edition is still that by J. G. T. Graesse (Leipzig: Libraria Arnoldiana, 1850). See also J. E. Gillet, "Traces of the Judas Legend in Spain," *Revue Hispanique*, XLV (1952), 316–41, and Paul Franklin Baum, "The Medieval Legend of Judas Iscariot," *PMLA*, XXXI (1916), 481–632; but note that neither author notices the San Pedro reference.

12. There are at least three distinct versions of the Veronica story, of which San Pedro rejects the least realistic and genuinely apocryphal version, to be found in the apocryphal *Mors Pilati* and *Vindicta Salvatoris*, ed. by C. Tischendorf in *Evangelia apocrypha* (Leipzig: Avenarius et Mendelssohn, 1853), the version popularized by the *Legenda aurea*. It is in any case difficult to classify this matter as genuinely apocryphal, since the relic conserved in Rome since the eighth century was declared by sundry Popes starting with Sixtus IV (1471–1484) to be authentic and the episode became one of the standard Stations of the Cross. For further bibliography, see my "The Supposed Sources . . ." and Rodríguez-Puértolas, "Leyendas cristianas primitivas en las obras de Fray Íñigo de Mendoza," *De la Edad Media . . . (cit. supra)*, pp. 101–20.

13. The inextricable intertwining of the Passion of Christ with the *Compassio Mariae* is typically Franciscan, and in this San Pedro and the Franciscans depart completely from the traditions associated with the *Devotio moderna*. San Pedro's adherence to the Franciscan Marianist tradition was probably one reason for his continued popularity in post-Tridentine Spain.

14. It may be read in any of the earlier *Opera omnia* of Bonaventure; it is excluded (properly) by Migne from his *Patrologia latina*. Apart from numerous editions printed elsewhere, there were at least four Spanish editions before 1499. See Dorothy Severin, introduction, Section II, to *La Pasión trobada . . . según la versión del Cancionero de Oñate-Castañeda.*

15. See I Corinthians 2, 2: "For I determined not to know any thing among you, save Jesus Christ, and him crucified." It is picked up and amplified by St. Bernard of Clairvaux (by whom the author of the *Meditationes* is very much influenced) in his *Sermo XLIII in Cantic., Patrologia latina*, 183, col. 995.

16. We know that St. Francis "dramatized" his own sermons by acting the dialogue, using miming gestures, etc. See Émile Mâle (who also has much to say about the iconographical influence of the *Meditationes*), *L'art religieux de la fin du moyen âge en France*, 5th revised ed. (Paris: A. Colin, 1949), p. 36. And see also G. R. Owst, *Literature and Pulpit in Medieval England* (Cambridge: Cambridge University Press, 1933; repr. Oxford: Blackwell, 1961), especially Chapter VIII, "Sermon and Drama."

17. See Julio Urquijo e Ibarra, "Del teatro litúrgico en el País Vasco: 'La Pasión trobada' de Diego de San Pedro," *Revue Internationale des Etudes Basques*, XXII (1931), 150–218. Dorothy Severin, " 'La Passión trobada' . . . y sus relaciones con el drama medieval," *cit. supra*, note 10, has calculated that, ignoring the introduction (to the nun), there are 1054 stanzas of narrative, 973 of dialogue, and 213 of comment by the author.

18. Charlotte M. Stern, "Fray Íñigo de Mendoza and Medieval Dramatic Ritual," *Hispanic Review*, XXXIII (1965), 197–245, believes that the episode of the shepherds in the *Vita Christi* is evidence of a dramatic tradition in Spain, and, indeed, refers repeatedly to "Mendoza's play," "Mendoza's *auto*," "Mendoza's Christmas pageant," etc. I find her argument, since she fails to refer to sermons, wholly unconvincing.

19. Dorothy Severin, " 'La Passión trobada' . . . y sus relaciones con el drama medieval," *cit.* in note 10, has shown that numerous parallels exist between San Pedro's *Passion* and medieval Passion plays in French, German, and English. The similarities can easily be attributed to common sources: after all, even a hypothetical medieval cycle of Passion plays in Spanish could hardly derive from similar plays in English or German. It could even be suggested that the popularity of San Pedro's *Passion* argues the rarity or nonexistence of dramatic sources.

20. It may be read in the late version of *The Passion* printed in *BAE*, XXXV (Madrid, 1872), 368–84.

21. Michel Darbord, *La poésie religieuse espagnole des Rois Catholiques à Philippe II* (Paris: Institut d'Études Hispaniques, 1965), pp. 101–6.

22. The work by Owst (*cit.* in note 16) contains a great deal of detailed information on mendicant preaching.

23. See Norman Cohn, *The Pursuit of the Millennium* (London: Secker, 1957).

24. See the most interesting and useful introduction by Rodney M. Thomson to his edition of *Tractatus Garsiae or The Translation of the Relics of SS. Gold and Silver*, Textus Minores XLVI (Leiden: Brill, 1973).

25. As I have argued elsewhere (in "The Supposed Sources . . . ," *cit.* in note 6), this movement could have had no real impact in Spain before the last decade of the fifteenth century. For information about it, see Albert Hyma, *The Christian Renaissance* (Grand Rapids, Michigan: The Reformed Press, 1924) and his *The "Devotio Moderna"* (Grand Rapids, Michigan: The Reformed Press, n.d.).

26. For a comprehensive list of early works on the Passion, in verse and in prose, and in Catalan, Portuguese, and Castilian, see Dorothy Severin, introduction, Part III, note 2, to *La Pasión trobada . . . según la versión del Cancionero de Oñate-Castañeda* (*cit. supra* note 2).

27. For the very important influence on Christian iconography of the *Meditationes*, see Mâle, *op. cit.* in note 16.

28. The miracle of Longinus's recovery of his sight may derive from a mistranslation of John 19, 35: *Et qui vidit, testimonium perhibuit* ("And he that saw *it* bare record"), but it was in any case confirmed by Decretal 417 of Pope Innocent III, in the thirteenth century. The emerging, but at this period still confused, tradition of the Stations of the Cross almost certainly helped to conserve the episode of Veronica. See Herbert Thurston, S. J., *The Stations of the Cross* (London: Burns and Oates, 1906; 1914).

29. For the history of Mendoza's *Vita Christi* see the works cited in note 7.

30. The four lines on San Pedro are actually included by José Simón Díaz as an item in his bibliography of critical works on San Pedro: *Bibliografía de la literatura hispánica*, III, *volumen* 2, revised ed. (Madrid: C. S. I. C., 1965), No. 6355, 420.

31. *Ni sé hazer la passión como hizo Diego / de Sanpedro, y después Cárcel de amores / que lo vno parecía oración de ciego / y lo otro cuento para cauadores, Los nueue libros de las Hauidas* (Zaragoza: Juan Millán, 1566), f. 10v–11r. There is an edition and

study by F. González Ollé: Jerónimo Arbolanche, *Las Abidas*, 2 vols. (Madrid: C. S. I. C., 1972). The facsimile reproduction of the text is paginated, and the verses appear on pp. 362–63.

32. *Antología de poetas líricos*, 13 vols. (Madrid: Viuda de Hernando, 1890–1908); Edición Nacional, 10 vols. (Santander: Aldus, 1944–1945), III, 182.

33. See p. XXXV of the 1950 ed., *Esta obra de coplero vulgar, carece de méritos literarios para que la reimpresión de sus largas tiradas de versos pueda interesar a los lectores de hoy.*

34. *Diálogo de la doctrina cristiana* (Alcalá, 1529); facsimile with introduction by Marcel Bataillon (Coimbra: Imprensa da Universidade, 1925), f. 95v: *esotras ymaginaciones que algunos tienen por contemplaciones, yo no sé qué son, ni qué fruto sacan dellas.*

35. It is in *BAE*, XVII, 401–501, but the best edition is that of Sister Mary Helen Patricia Corcoran (Washington: Catholic University of America, 1935). Frank Pierce has published a partial edition with a useful introduction (Salamanca: Anaya, 1971).

Chapter Four

1. A bibliography of the Latin sources may be found in Mâle, *L'art religieux, cit. supra,* pp. 118–21. Although the entire work contains not a single reference to Diego de San Pedro, the reader may consult with profit Pierre Le Gentil, *La poésie lyrique espagnole et portugaise à la fin du moyen âge*, Vol. I: *Les thèmes et les genres* (Rennes: Plihon, 1949), Book VI: "La poésie religieuse," and especially Chapter I: "La chanson pieuse," pp. 297–324.

2. Alfonso X, *Cantigas de Santa María*, ed. Marqués de Valmar, 2 vols. (Madrid: Real Academia Española, 1889) or ed. Walter Mettmann, 3 vols. (Coimbra: Imprensa da Universidade, 1959–1964).

3. It is No. 344 in *Cancionero de Baena*, ed. José M. Azáceta (Madrid: C. S. I. C., 1966).

4. The *Stabat Mater* antecedes the *Cantigas* of Alfonso X if it was written by Pope Innocent III (d. 1216), but it has also been ascribed to the Franciscan Jacopone da Todi (d. 1306), in which case its priority must be dubious. There are, however, other occurrences of the image: this is simply the best known. The lines I cite were translated by E. Carwell as "For her soul of joy bereavèd, / Bow'd with anguish, deeply grievèd, / Felt the sharp and piercing sword" (*Hymns Ancient and Modern*, No. 117).

5. It may be read in the *Cancionero castellano del siglo XV*, ed. by R. Foulché-Delbosc, II, *NBAE* 22 (Madrid: Bailly-Baillière, 1915), 91–92. It should be noted that the text printed there is no

more than a copy of the edition of the *Cancionero* of Gómez Manrique prepared by A. Paz y Melia, 2 vols. (Madrid: A. Pérez Dubrull, 1885), a work now much less accessible than Foulché-Delbosc's.

6. The first person to spot the coincidences was Prof. Edward M. Wilson, who abandoned his own article on the subject and passed his materials to me in 1957.

7. For more detailed discussion, see my "The Religious Poems of Diego de San Pedro: Their Relationship and Their Dating," *Hispanic Review*, XXVIII (1960), 1–15, and especially 10–11.

8. As I have indicated, it is possible—and, I believe, probable—that Gómez Manrique's poem has priority in time; but there is a very great distance between Don Gómez's brief and primitive lyric and San Pedro's ample, structured work.

9. It may be read in *Cancionero castellano del siglo XV*, II, 313 (see note 5).

10. See Vol. I of my ed. of the *Obras completas*, 150–65.

11. This is the *cancionero* in which is also to be found the first known printing of *The Versified Passion*. See my "The First Printing of San Pedro's *Passión trobada*," *Hispanic Review*, XXX (1962), 149–51.

12. Since they have never been reprinted elsewhere, I include them in my edition of *Arnalte and Lucenda* (*Obras completas*, I), and they may be found on pp. 157 and 161.

13. For the two versions, see my -edition and the Appendix of Variants (*Obras completas*, I).

14. Some details about this now lost work were extracted by Gallardo from the "Abecedarium Bibliothecae Colombinae," where it is entered as "Las siete angustias de Nuestra Señora por Jacobi de Sampedro." See Gallardo, *Ensayo de una biblioteca española de libros raros y curiosos*, 4 vols. (Madrid: Rivadeneyra and Tello, 1863–1889), *s.v.* San Pedro.

15. The only copy known to exist is in the British Museum, C.63. f. 10. The dating was done by Sir Henry Thomas.

16. See Regula Langbehn-Rohland, *Zur Interpretation der Romane des Diego de San Pedro* (Heidelberg: Carl Winter Universitätsverlag, 1970), p. 143, where she casts doubt on the severe, dismissive criticism of Samonà, *il cattivo gusto e la poca sensibilità verso l'intima coerenza del racconto . . . un atteggiamento inesperto . . . freddo accademismo,* etc. See Carmelo Samonà, "Diego de San Pedro: dall'Arnalte y Lucenda alla Cárcel de Amor," *Studi in onore di Pietro Silva* (Florence: Felice le Monnier, 1957), pp. 261–77.

Chapter Five

1. I do not translate *tratado* as "treatise"; I find unconvincing the thesis of Anna Krause, "El 'tractado' novelístico de Diego de San Pedro," *Bulletin Hispanique*, LIV (1952), 245–75, which would make San Pedro's fiction didactic in intent. While there are no doubt some didactic elements to be found in his two stories, it is obvious that in the fifteenth and sixteenth centuries the term *tratado* was used in a very loose and unspecialized sense, and that it is much more accurately translated as "story," "romance," or even "novel." The "didactic treatise" interpretation of *tratado* has been picked up by Dinko Cvitanovic in "El tratadismo en Juan Rodríguez del Padrón," *Cuadernos del Sur*, II (July, 1969–June, 1971 [1972]), 25–36. He sees San Pedro and Juan de Flores as moving further away from Juan Rodríguez's *tratadismo*, but finds the didactic element a "constant" in all "sentimental novels."

2. The date can be established really only for the verses in praise of Isabella, but must be a reasonably approximate date for the novel as a whole. For the details of the argument, see my introduction to Vol. I of San Pedro's *Obras completas*, pp. 44–47.

3. J. Rubió Balaguer, *Los personajes viven en constante monólogo*: see the preface to his ed. of *Cárcel de Amor* (Barcelona: Gustavo Gili, 1941), p. 8.

4. Every one of the letters and most of the speeches in both of San Pedro's novels obey the rules of the manuals of letter writing, in which it is laid down that the one indispensable section in any letter is the *petitio*. While this prescription may have some basis in reality, it is also explicable historically as a relic of the never-questioned notion that the art of rhetoric is the art of persuasion. See section III below for further detail.

5. For details, the reader may consult Heinrich Lausberg, *Handbuch der literarischen Rhetorik: Eine Grundlegung der Literaturwissenschaft* (Munich: Max Hüber Verlag, 1960); Spanish translation by José Pérez Riesco, *Manual de retórica literaria: Fundamentos de una ciencia de la literatura*, 3 vols. (Madrid: Gredos, 1966–1968).

6. See Lausberg, *op. cit.*, paragraph 823.

7. *Obras completas*, I, 183.

8. *Obras completas*, II, 166–67 and 170.

9. There are a multitude of different ways of defining what precisely constituted "the Renaissance"; but the writer's consciousness of actively contributing to some sort of rebirth is certainly one of the most crucial.

10. See Charles E. Kany, *The Beginnings of the Epistolary Novel*

in France, Italy and Spain (Berkeley: University of California Press, 1937).

11. For more precise details of how and when the *artes dictaminis* became known in Castile, see Charles Faulhaber, *Latin Rhetorical Theory in Thirteenth and Fourteenth Century Castile* (Berkeley: University of California Press, 1972), especially pp. 103–21. Note that in classical Rome there is no evidence for letter writing being taught in the schools before the third century.

12. There is a very large bibliography of works devoted wholly or in part to the *artes dictaminis*; see James J. Murphy, *Medieval Rhetoric: A Select Bibliography* (Toronto: University of Toronto Press, 1971), pp. 55–70. I have listed half a dozen of the most useful and summarized what is important for the study of Diego de San Pedro in the introduction to Vol. II of his *Obras completas*, 52–55.

13. See Lausberg, *op. cit.*, paragraphs 263–88.

14. For the importance of the work in the development of six-teenth-century English prose style, see W. G. Crane, *Wit and Rhetoric in the Renaissance: The Formal Basis of Elizabethan Prose Style* (New York: Columbia University Press, 1937).

15. There are in fact fifteen, but all the standard editions query the attribution of No. 15 (Sappho) to Ovid.

16. See Ovid, *Amores*, II, 18, 27–28.

17. See Kany, *op. cit.*, pp. 16–18, for further details.

18. *Obras completas*, I, 88.

19. See Langbehn-Rohland, *op. cit.*, p. 128.

20. See the introduction to Vol. II of the *Obras completas*, p. 15.

21. Rudolph Schevill, *Ovid and the Renascence in Spain* (Berkeley: University of California Press, 1913; repr. Hildesheim: Georg Olms Verlag, 1971), p. 117.

22. I have looked at contemporary misunderstanding of San Pedro's intentions in "Nicolás Núñez's Continuation of the *Cárcel de Amor*," *Studies in Spanish Literature of the Golden Age Presented to Edward M. Wilson* (London: Tamesis Books, 1973), pp. 357–66.

23. The tale was printed in a numerous series of editions of his *Opera omnia* (I have used that of Bâle, 1551), but, since its author condemned it when he became Pope Pius II, one frequently finds that early censors have cut it out, i.e., literally, with a knife. A Spanish translation, now lost, was printed at Salamanca in 1491. The earliest extant Spanish version is the *Hystoria muy verdadera de dos amantes Eurialo franco y Lucrecia senesa fecha por Eneas Silvio* (Seville: Cromberger, 1512) which R. Foulché-Delbosc transcribed and printed (Barcelona: L'Avenç, 1907).

24. In a paper entitled "Language and Tragedy in Góngora's

Píramo y Tisbe" given to the Association of Hispanists of Great Britain and Ireland at Hull in March, 1973, subsequently circulated in cyclostyled copies and retitled "Some Preliminary Remarks to a Study of Góngora's *Fábula de Píramo y Tisbe.*" See also his *Two Versions of Pyramus and Thisbe: Jorge de Montemayor and Sánchez de Viana*, Exeter Hispanic Texts IX (Exeter: Exeter University Press, forthcoming 1974).

25. See Ovid, *Metamorphoses*, IV, 121–24.

26. Cf. the suicide of Pyramus, the drowning of Ceyx (XI, 566–67), the sacrifice of Polyxena (XIII, 479), etc., etc.

27. For a discussion of the problem in terms somewhat different from mine, see E. V. Rieu's introduction to his translation of Apollonius of Rhodes, *The Voyage of Argo* (Harmondsworth: Penguin Books, 1959; 1971). He refers to "humorous remarks" on p. 13.

28. For the medieval misinterpretations of Ovid see E. K. Rand, *Ovid and His Influence* (Boston: Marshall Jones, 1927), the penultimate chapter devoted to Ovid in the Middle Ages by L. P. Wilkinson in his *Ovid Recalled* (Cambridge: Cambridge University Press, 1955) and Rudolph Schevill, *op. cit.*

29. As, for instance, in John Gower's *Confessio amantis*, Book III, which deals with the sin of anger. The Confessor tells the poet (verses 1495–1502) that the moral of the story is self-betrayal through foolish haste. In some of the medieval moralized versions of Ovid the story was told as a religious allegory: Pyramus is Christ, Thisbe the human soul, and the lion the defiling power of Evil.

30. See Schevill, *op. cit.*, pp. 107–13.

31. For some later developments of the conceit, see R. O. Jones, "Renaissance Butterfly, Mannerist Flea: Tradition and Change in Renaissance Poetry," *Modern Language Notes*, 80 (1965), 166–84.

32. Shakespeare, of course, abuses the story in a not wholly dissimilar way in *A Midsummer Night's Dream*.

33. *Orígenes de la novela, ed. cit.*, II, Chapter VI.

34. P. E. Russell objects strenuously to the term, preferring "courtly romance" (at least for San Pedro's stories), in "Spanish Literature (1474–1681)," *Spain: A Companion to Spanish Studies*, ed. P. E. Russell (London: Methuen, 1973), pp. 270–71.

35. Some recent attempts to define the genre may be found in José Luis Varela, "Revisión de la novela sentimental," *Revista de Filología Española*, XLVIII (1965 [1967]), 351–82; Regula Langbehn-Rohland, *op. cit.*, pp. 22–23; A. D. Deyermond, *A Literary History of Spain: The Middle Ages* (London: Ernest Benn; New York: Barnes and Noble, 1971), p. 162; and, for similar works in Catalan, Arseni

Pacheco, introduction to *Novel·lettes sentimentals dels segles XIV i XV* (Barcelona: Edicions 62, 1972), pp. 8 ff.

36. Armando Durán, *Estructura y técnicas de la novela sentimental y caballeresca* (Madrid: Gredos, 1973), especially pp. 60–63.

37. Note that *Sátira* is not translatable in any neat way; it does not mean "satire" and there is nothing satirical about the work: the term is misused by the Condestable to indicate that he uses a mixture of verse and prose to tell the story.

38. Full bibliographical details would unnecessarily overweight these notes; references to the various editions may be found in Langbehn-Rohland, *op. cit.*, but note that she is in error about the date of the first printing of Nicolás Núñez's continuation of *Prison of Love*, having been misled by the British Museum catalogue.

39. Agustín Millares Carlo, *Literatura española hasta fines del siglo XV* (Mexico: Robredo, 1950), p. 294: "Está caracterizada por su índole autobiográfica, mezcla patente de elementos relacionados con la vida del autor, *principio fundamental del género*" (my italics).

40. See note 1 above.

41. M. R. Lida, "Juan Rodríguez del Padrón: influencia," *Nueva Revista de Filología Hispánica*, VIII (1954), 1–38, believes that San Pedro is clearly indebted to Juan Rodríguez, but her evidence is exceedingly slender: she can point only to quite trivial coincidences, such as the insertion of verse in a prose narrative (*Arnalte and Lucenda*) or the use of allegory as an introduction (*Prison of Love*), and the hypothesis seems to me both unnecessary and unlikely.

42. For the importance of such writers as Guillaume de Machaut and Christine de Pisan, see the introduction to Vol. I of *Obras completas*, 55–56.

43. For an analysis of some of the major differences, see Pamela Waley, "Love and Honour in the *novelas sentimentales* of Diego de San Pedro and Juan de Flores," *Bulletin of Hispanic Studies*, XLIII (1966), 253–75.

44. See Schevill, *op. cit.*, especially pp. 117–18.

45. *Ars amatoria*, I, 615–16: *saepe tamen vere coepit simulator amare; / saepe, quod incipiens finxerat esse, fuit.*

46. *Obras completas*, I, 103–5.

47. For *narratio* as a variety of *digressio*, see Lausberg, *op. cit.*, paragraphs 290–92.

48. *Obras completas*, I, 111.

49. See my "Diego de San Pedro's Stylistic Reform," *Bulletin of Hispanic Studies*, XXXVII (1960), 1–15.

Chapter Six

1. For a discussion of the dating of the *Sermon*, see the introduction to *Obras completas*, I, 41, and for the Spanish text, the same volume, 173–83.

2. Although the whole verse will be sought in vain in the Bible, San Pedro has made use of genuine biblical phrases: cf. Luke 21, 19; I Peter 2, 19; II Maccabees 6, 30, etc.

3. There is a very extensive bibliography on the *artes praedicandi*, of which over three hundred survive in MS. Among the most useful works are two books by G. R. Owst, *Preaching in Medieval England* (Cambridge: Cambridge University Press, 1926) and *Literature and Pulpit in Medieval England*, 2nd ed. (Oxford: Blackwell, 1961), and the standard work by Th.-M. Charland, *Artes praedicandi: Contribution à l'histoire de la rhétorique au moyen âge* (Paris and Ottawa: Institut d'Études Médiévales d'Ottawa, 1936). For further references, see Murphy, *op. cit.*

4. See *Obras completas*, II, 33–34.

5. "Courtly love" is too vast a topic to embark on here. I touch on it again in Chapter 7, but for a fuller account, with a bibliography of some more recent and important works, see *Obras completas*, II, 7–43.

6. For medical views on love and further references, see *Obras completas*, II, 13–15.

7. See Peter Dronke, *Medieval Latin and the Rise of European Love-Lyric*, 2 vols. (Oxford: Clarendon Press, 1965), I, especially 9–10.

Chapter Seven

1. For an interpretation of the role of the hairy savage in various medieval works, including *Prison of Love*, see A. D. Deyermond, "El hombre salvaje en la novela sentimental," *Filología*, X (1964), 97–111, and for real-life *caballeros salvajes* (knights who dressed as savages and invited combat), see Martín de Riquer, *Vida caballeresca en la España del siglo XV* (Madrid: Real Academia Española, 1965).

2. See *Obras completas*, II, 80.

3. Leriano, of course, betrays himself and Laureola by the involuntary signs of emotion which San Pedro warned against in his *Sermon*.

4. See *Obras completas*, II, 117. San Pedro excuses himself from describing the combat at length, saying, *por no detenerme en esto que parece cuento de historias viejas* ("so as not to dally over what must seem like something from an ancient tale"). Gili Gaya in a footnote,

ed. cit., suggests that this is a reference to the romances of chivalry; it is also possible that San Pedro refers to the fight in this way since such formal duels before the king had not been for a long time part of the Spanish scene.

5. Wardropper, in "El mundo sentimental . . . ," attempts to sketch the "character" of the king, pp. 177–78, but confesses, p. 186, that we do not know his motive for interrupting the duel. Márquez Villanueva, *art. cit.*, thinks him simply cruel, unjust, and culpable. I am more inclined to dismiss the "character" of the king and his implausible actions as no more than a narrative device necessary to create the crisis.

6. For the history of the "harsh law of Scotland," see Barbara Matulka, *The Novels of Juan de Flores and Their European Diffusion* (New York: Columbia University Press, 1931), pp. 55 ff.

7. *Obras completas*, I, 149.

8. For the history of the feminist debate, see Barbara Matulka, *op. cit.*; José Francisco Gatti, *Contribución al estudio de la "Cárcel de amor": La apología de Leriano* (Buenos Aires: unsigned, 1955); and Jacob Ormstein, "La misoginia y el profeminismo en la literatura castellana," *Revista de Filología Hispánica*, III (1941), 219–32.

9. The debate is a major feature of Flores's romance and is advertised in the title of the first known edition: *Historia de Grisel y Mirabella con la disputa de Torrellas y Braçayda* (. . . *with the Debate between Torrellas and Braçayda*). Torrellas's victory brings about the death of both the lovers.

10. *Obras completas*, II, 155.

11. San Pedro does achieve some pathetic effects with some simple phrases, but the *planctus* is also a highly-wrought rhetorical set piece. See *Obras completas*, II, 58–59. I quote the phrase used by Ian Michael in his contribution to *Spain: A Companion . . .* , (*cit. supra*), p. 237.

12. Even of allegorical castles and prisons there is an abundance of examples; see Regula Langbehn-Rohland, *op. cit.*, pp. 151–53.

13. Shakespeare, Sonnet CXVI.

14. I do not mean to imply that there were not also satirical, burlesque, or comic allegories.

15. On perfect and imperfect allegory, see *Obras completas*, II, 49–52, and Lausberg, *op. cit.*, paragraph 897.

16. The English translator, Lord Berners, found the transition so disconcerting that after "Sierra Morena" he inserted the phrase "in the country of Macedonia."

17. José Amador de los Ríos, *Historia crítica de la literatura española*, 7 vols. (Madrid: Rodríguez and Muñoz, 1861–1865), VI,

347–51, insists that the allegory does not stop when the story starts "really and actively," that the Author's role parallels that of Dante in the *Divina Commedia* (p. 349), and that the "fantastic happenings" in the work represent "true allegory"; but he is not using the term "allegory" in any accepted or acceptable medieval sense.

18. See the stimulating article (with which I do not entirely agree) by Bruce W. Wardropper, "Allegory and the Role of 'el Autor' in the 'Cárcel de amor,' " *Philological Quarterly*, XXXI (1952), 39–44.

19. See Gerhart Hoffmeister, "Diego de San Pedro und Hans Ludwig von Kufstein," *Arcadia*, VI (1971), 139–50. (Leriano becomes Constante.)

20. For instance, Arnald of Vilanova in his *De amore heroico*. See John Livingston Lowes, "The Loveres Maladye of Hereos," *Modern Philology*, X (1913–1914), 491–546.

21. On what was in the earlier part of the fifteenth century a very clear conflict between arms and letters, see N. G. Round, "Renaissance Culture and its Opponents in Fifteenth-century Castile," *Modern Language Review*, LVII (1962), 204–15, and P. E. Russell, "Fifteenth-century Lay Humanism," in *Spain: A Companion . . .*, (*cit. supra*), pp. 237–42.

22. This does not emerge from Arnalte's challenge to Elierso, or from anything he says or does, but he does report briefly that he was informed by one of Lucenda's women that she had married under pressure from her family: *Obras completas*, I, 142.

23. *Amadis of Gaul*, the best-known and possibly the best of the Spanish romances of chivalry, was written in the fourteenth century but rewritten about 1492 for printing in 1508.

24. Dante, *Vita nuova*, XXVIII–XLII.

25. He speaks of *el lugar donde van las almas desesperadas*, *Obras completas*, II, 108. Various writers of the late fifteenth century do in fact speak of suicide without censure; see Erna Ruth Berndt, *Amor, Muerte, y Fortuna en "La Celestina"* (Madrid: Gredos, 1963), pp. 112–14. For the earlier conflict of authorities, see Abelard's *Sic et non*, in *Patrologia latina*, CLXXVIII.

26. There is no satisfactory modern edition of Nicolás Núñez's *tratado*; the text transcribed and printed by Menéndez Pelayo in *Orígenes*, II (1st ed.), is sadly corrupt. I hope shortly to publish an edition of it.

27. Wardropper, "El mundo sentimental . . . ," says that Leriano's goal (*objeto central*) is to marry Laureola; it is possible that San Pedro did assume something of the sort, but he failed to make it clear.

28. *Procedit usque ad oris osculum, lacertique amplexum et verecundum amantis nudae contactum, extremo praetermisso solatio,*

p. 93 in Andreas Capellanus, *De amore*, ed. Amadeo Pagès (Castellón de la Plana: Sociedad Castellonense de Cultura, 1930).

29. A. D. Deyermond, in *A Literary History of Spain: The Middle Ages* (*cit. supra*), says "San Pedro . . . sharpens the tragedy by making Laureola reciprocate Leriano's love," p. 165; Wardropper, "El mundo sentimental . . . ," speaks of her cruelty, p. 175; Gili Gaya says she is ungrateful (*la ingrata Laureola*, p. IX) and cruel (p. XIV).

30. Laureola is quite explicit about the malice of the masses, *Obras completas*, II, 153.

31. See Notes 6 and 9 above.

32. For a different view, interpreting the story in terms of the conflict of codes, see Wardropper, "El mundo sentimental."

33. *Obras completas*, II, 80; it should be noted that the syntax is not completely unambiguous: it could be the Alcaide de los Donceles who thought the style of the *Sermon* superior.

34. See the latter part of my "Diego de San Pedro's Stylistic Reform."

35. I have no space to deal with *abbreviatio* here; see the article cited in the previous note.

36. *Argumentatio* is the technical term one would use for Leriano's defense of women; see Lausberg, paragraphs 348–430, and *Obras completas*, II, 57.

37. For a study of the origin of the idea of and the desire for a personal style (though I cannot accept much of what he says), see Juan Marichal, *Voluntad de estilo* (Barcelona: Seix Barral, 1957).

38. On the methods of *amplificatio*, consult Edmond Faral, *Les arts poétiques du XIIe et du XIIIe siècle* (Paris: Champion, 1924; 1958), pp. 61 ff. and 99–103.

39. For the "colors of rhetoric," see Leonid Arbusow, *Colores rhetorici: Eine Auswahl rhetorischer Figuren und Gemeinplätze als Hilfsmittel für Übungen an mittelalterlichen Texten* (Göttingen: Vandenhoeck and Ruprecht, 1948; 1963).

40. I take these nice examples from Christopher Hohler, "Kings and Castles: Court Life in Peace and War," *The Middle Ages*, ed. Joan Evans (London: Thames and Hudson, 1966), pp. 133–78.

41. For its influence in shaping Baldesar Castiglione's conception of the perfect courtier, see A. Giannini, "La 'Cárcel de Amor' y el 'Cortegiano' de B. Castiglione," *Revue Hispanique*, XLVI (1919), 545–68.

42. It is frequently said that *Prison of Love* owed its success to its female readers: Menéndez Pelayo, *Antología*, Ed. Nac., III, 176, envisages it concealed in the workbaskets of "matrons and maids"

(*dueñas y doncellas*), and various critics and historians have converted this fancy into "fact." There is, however, some basis for the supposition that *Prison of Love* did have a special appeal to women readers, for Luis Vives, Fray Luis de Granada, and Fray Pedro Malón de Chaide all lament its disastrous effect on young women, who prefer it to books of devotion.

Chapter Eight

1. The text may be found in *Obras completas*, I, 93–100.

2. For the historical background, see Chapter 1.

3. The earlier poems are mentioned by R. Menéndez Pidal, *Poesía juglaresca y orígenes de las literaturas románicas*, 6th ed. (Madrid: Espasa-Calpe, 1957), pp. 134–88 (omit an intermediate section on poems of abuse), and the later ones are listed by Pierre Le Gentil, *La poésie lyrique*, (*cit. supra*), I, Book VIII, Chapter I: "Le panégyrique," 437. Le Gentil says "all" these poems are accompanied by requests, but there are exceptions, including San Pedro's poem.

4. See Lausberg, *op. cit.*, paragraphs 240–45, and for further details on Castilian panegyric and panegyrists, see *Obras completas*, III, introduction.

5. This is "El mayor bien de quereros," which I analyze and interpret in the introduction to *Obras completas*, III. Gracián's commentary may be read in Baltasar Gracián, *Agudeza y arte de ingenio*, ed. Evaristo Calderón, 2 vols. (Madrid: Castalia, 1969), in *Discurso* XXIV, I, 236–46.

6. *Hilo* is normally "thread," but that seems a very odd gift, and the other sense was current.

7. See my "Hacia una interpretación y apreciación de las canciones del *Cancionero general* de 1511," *Filología*, XIII (1968–1969), 361–81.

8. I owe this interesting example to Prof. E. M. Wilson; see *The Works of Sir John Suckling: The Non-Dramatic Works*, ed. Thomas Clayton (Oxford: Clarendon Press, 1971), No. 16, p. 19.

Chapter Nine

1. For the text of *Contempt of Fortune*, see *Obras completas*, III, and for a fuller discussion of the history of Fortune, the introduction, which depends heavily but not exclusively on Howard R. Patch, *The Goddess Fortuna in Medieval Literature* (Cambridge, Mass.: Harvard University Press, 1927).

2. Ovid, *Tristia*, V, 8, 18.

3. Seneca, *De constantia sapientiae*, V, 2.

4. As, for instance, in *De civitate Dei*, V, 9.

5. Apart from sundry remarks in the *Summa theologica*, St. Thomas deals at length with chance and causality in his *Commentarium Physicorum Aristotelis*.

6. See, for instance, Jerome's commentary on Ecclesiasticus in Migne, *Patrologia latina*, XXIII, col. 1085.

7. See his *Divina Commedia: Inferno*, lines 67–96.

8. See H. R. Patch, *The Tradition of Boethius: A Study of His Importance in Medieval Culture* (Oxford and New York: Oxford University Press, 1935).

9. For more specific information on the use of his sources, see *Obras completas*, III.

10. For a much fuller discussion and assessment of *Contempt of Fortune*, see the introduction to *Obras completas*, III.

Chapter Ten

1. I have listed a long series of such remarks in the section "La personalidad literaria de San Pedro," *Obras completas*, III.

2. It is hard to overestimate the importance of the Latin background for medieval literature. I have preached about this at length in *Spanish Literary Historiography: Three Forms of Distortion* (Exeter: Exeter University Press, 1967).

Selected Bibliography

PRIMARY SOURCES

Obras completas. 3 vols. (Madrid: Castalia, 1972–   ): I, *Arnalte y Lucenda* and *Sermón*, ed. Keith Whinnom, 1973; II, *Cárcel de Amor*, ed. K. W., 1972; III, *Poesías*, ed. K. W. and Dorothy S. Severin, forthcoming. This is the only complete edition of the works of San Pedro, and contains the only annotated editions of *The Passion* and the minor verse.

Obras [Selected Works] (Madrid: Espasa-Calpe, 1950; 1958; 1967). Ed. Samuel Gili Gaya. Omits *La Pasión trovada* and one short obscene poem. Reprints the often incomprehensible text of *Arnalte y Lucenda* of Burgos, 1491. Gili Gaya's work was plagiarized without acknowledgment by Jaime Uyá (Barcelona: Ediciones Zeus, 1969) and by Arturo Souto Alabarce (Mexico: Porrúa, 1971): the texts, including misprints and omissions, are identical.

La Pasión trovada. Apart from the early MS. version in the "Cancionero de Oñate-Castañeda" (in private hands), there are four early extant printings of *La Pasión* which are independent of one another. For the MS. version, see Dorothy S. Severin, *La Passión trobada de Diego de San Pedro: Edición paleográfica, según la versión manuscrita de Oñate-Castañeda* (Naples: Istituto Universitario Orientale di Napoli, 1974). For the text of the earliest extant *pliego suelto*, known as *PT* 1 (Salamanca?: Hutz and Sanz?, 1496?), see Antonio Pérez Gómez's facsimile in *Tercera floresta de incunables* (Valencia, 1958), his photographic reproduction, or Julio Urquijo's transcription (see below: Secondary Sources). All five of the early redactions of the poem, including that of the *cancionero* done by Hurus in Zaragoza in 1495, *PT* 2 (Burgos?: Juan de Junta?, 1530?), and *PT* 3 (Lisbon?: Germão Galharde?, 1530?), none of which has been reproduced in any form, are taken into account in the edition prepared for Vol. III of San Pedro's *Obras completas* (see the first item above). The text in Biblioteca de Autores Españoles XXXV, *Romancero y cancionero sagrados* (Madrid: Rivadeneyra, 1872, and frequent reprintings), pp. 368–84, derives from an eighteenth-century edition. There were numerous printed editions of *La Pasión trovada*, running into the second half of the nineteenth century; for these, see the bibliography in *Obras completas*, III. No translation exists.

Las siete angustias de Nuestra Señora. The version which was printed in the 1491 edition of *Arnalte y Lucenda* may be found in the three editions of selected works by San Pedro (see the second item above). The version with additional stanzas, which appeared along with *La Pasión trovada* in the Hurus *cancionero*, and an unsigned and undated *pliego* of c. 1540, are taken into account in reproducing the poem in *Arnalte y Lucenda* in Vol. I of the *Obras completas*. The poem was omitted from the translations of *Arnalte y Lucenda*.

Arnalte y Lucenda. Tractado de amores de Arnalte a [*sic*] *Lucenda* (Burgos: Fadrique Alemán de Basilea, 1491). Facsimile with a prologue by A. G. de Amezúa (Madrid: Real Academia Española, 1952). This text is the one used by Gili Gaya in preparing his edition (see item 2 above).

Tratado de Arnalte y Lucenda (Burgos: Alonso de Melgar, 1522). This is the text transcribed by R. Foulché-Delbosc in *Revue Hispanique* (see below: Secondary Sources). Two further Spanish editions known to have existed are now lost. The two extant editions are independent one of the other, and both were taken into account in preparing the edition of *Arnalte y Lucenda* in Vol. I of the *Obras completas.*

Arnalte y Lucenda: translations. French: by Nicholas d'Herberay, *L'amant mal traicté de sa mye*, subsequently retitled *Petit traité de Arnalte et Lucenda* (Paris?: Denis Janot?, 1539?). There were thereafter at least twelve monolingual reprintings of this translation. French and Italian: by Nicholas d'Herberay and Bartolome Maraffi, *Petit traité de Arnalte et Lucenda; Picciol trattato d'Arnalte e di Lucenda, intitolato L'amante mal trattato dalla sua amorosa* (Lyon: Balthazar Arnoullet, 1555). There were at least four reprintings of this bilingual edition. English (1): John Clerke, *A certayn treatye most wyttely deuised, orygynally written in the Spaynysshe, lately traducted in to Frenche entytled Lamant mal traicte de samye* (London: Robert Wyer, 1543); English (2) and Italian: by Claudius Hollyband (Claude de Sainliens) and Maraffi, *The pretie and wittie historie of Arnalt & Lucenda, with certen rules and dialogues set foorth for the learner of th'Italian tong*, subsequently retitled *The Italian schoole-maister. Containing rules for the perfect pronouncing of th'Italian tongue . . . and a fine Tuscan historie* called *Arnalt & Lucenda* (London: Thomas Purfoote, 1575; 1591; 1597; 1608); English (3): Leonard Lawrence, *A small treatise betwixt Arnalte and Lucenda entituled The evill-treated lover, or, The melancholy knight* (London: J. Okes, 1639). For further details, see Vol. I of *Obras completas.*

Sermón ordenado por Diego de Sant Pedro porque dixeron unas señoras que le desseavan oyr predicar (Burgos?: Juan de Junta?, 1540?). There are three other sixteenth-century printings, two together with *Prison of Love.* There are defective modern editions by M. Menéndez Pelayo, *Orígenes de la novela*, II (Madrid: Bailly-Baillière, 1907; see below, Secondary Sources, and note that the text is not reproduced in the Edición Nacional), and by Gili Gaya (see above). It appears in Vol. I of *Obras completas* where further bibliographical details may be found. No translation exists.

Cárcel de Amor (Seville: Cuatro compañeros alemanes, 1492). Facsimile by Antonio Pérez Gómez, Incunables Poéticos Castellanos, XIII (Valencia, 1967). With the continuation by Nicolás Núñez (Burgos: Fadrique Alemán de Basilea, 1496). There were thereafter at least twenty-two reprintings. There are modern editions by R. Foulché-Delbosc, Bibliotheca Hispanica, XV (Barcelona: L'Avenç, 1904), by Menéndez Pelayo, *Orígenes* (see under *Sermón*, above), and by Gili Gaya (see item 2 above), as well as half a dozen editions without scholarly pretensions which reproduce the texts of Menéndez Pelayo or Gili Gaya. For further bibliographical details, see Vol. II of *Obras completas.*

Cárcel de Amor: translations. Catalan: by Bernardi Vallmanya, *Lo Carcer de Amor* (Barcelona: Johan Rosenbach, 1493); facsimile by Lambert Mata (Barcelona: Vilanova y Geltrú, 1906). Italian: by Lelio de Manfredi, *Carcer d'amore* (Venice: Georgio de Rusconi, 1515); reprinted at least nine times. French: translator anonymous [François d'Assy], *La Prison d'amour* (Paris: Antonio Couteau, 1525); about seven reprintings. Bilingual edition, French (a different translator, anonymous) and Spanish: *Cárcel de Amor; Prison d'amour* (Paris: Gilles Corrozet, 1552); about fifteen reprintings. English: by John Bourchier, Lord Berners, *The Castell of Love* (London: R. Wyer?, 1549?; 1560?); facsimile by William G. Crane (see Secondary Sources). German: by Hans Ludwig von Kufstein, *Carcell de amor oder Gefängnis der Lieb* (Leipzig: Ochie, 1625); four times reprinted. For further bibliographical details see *Obras completas*, II.

Minor verse. All San Pedro's minor poems appeared in Hernando del Castillo's *Cancionero general*, twenty-two in the first edition

(Valencia: Cristóbal Kofman, 1511), and six more in the second (1514). Many reappear in other *cancioneros* and in *pliegos sueltos.* The first modern edition which collected the minor verse was Gili Gaya's *Obras*, although he deliberately omitted one obscene poem and some of doubtful attribution. They all appear in *Obras completas*, III, together with full bibliographical details.

Desprecio de la Fortuna. The earliest edition known appears in *Las CCC del famosíssimo poeta Juan de Mena con su glosa, y las cinqüenta con su glosa, y otras obras* (Zaragoza: George Coci, 1506; 1509). It also appears in Hernando del Castillo's *Cancionero general* (1511, see *Minor verse*, above), and in various other *cancioneros* and *pliegos sueltos.* The modern editions by Menéndez Pelayo, *Antología de poetas líricos*, V (1944; see below, Secondary Sources) and by Gili Gaya are based on the text in the *Cancionero general*, though Gili Gaya used the Mena anthology for the prose prologue, which is missing in Menéndez Pelayo's edition. It appears in *Obras completas*, III, where additional bibliographical detail may be found.

SECONDARY SOURCES

BERMEJO HURTADO, H., and CVITANOVIC, D. "El sentido de la aventura espiritual en la *Cárcel de Amor*," *Revista de Filología Española*, XLIX (1966 [1968]), 289–300. A jargon-ridden piece of criticism which does bring out the point that Leriano embarks knowingly upon a dangerous "spiritual adventure."

BERTONI, G. "Nota su Mario Equicola, bibliofilo e cortigiano," *Giornale Storico della Letteratura Italiana*, LXVI (1915), 281–83. Suggests that San Pedro influenced the thinking of this early sixteenth-century, semi-Neoplatonic theorist of love.

BORINSKI, LUDWIG. "Diego de San Pedro und die euphuistische Erzählung," *Anglia*, LXXXIX (1971), 224–39. Reexamines the influence of San Pedro on the style and form of Lyly's didactic romances and their imitations.

BUCETA, ERASMO. "Algunas relaciones de la 'Menina e Moça' con la literatura española, especialmente con las novelas de Diego de San Pedro," *Revista de la Biblioteca, Archivo y Museo del Ayuntamiento de Madrid*, X (1933), 291–307. On San Pedro's influence on Bernardim Ribeiro; suggests that *Cárcel de Amor* is the story of Don Pedro Girón and the Princess Isabella.

CIOCCHINI, HÉCTOR. "Hipótesis de un realismo mítico-alegórico en algunos catálogos de amantes (Juan Rodríguez del Padrón,

Garci-Sánchez de Badajoz, Diego de San Pedro, Cervantes),"
Revista de Filología Española, L (1967 [1970]), 299–306.
Possibly mere verbiage, but certainly beyond my comprehension.

COTARELO Y MORI, EMILIO. "Nuevos y curiosos datos biográficos del
famoso trovador y novelista Diego de San Pedro," *Boletín de la
Real Academia Española*, XIV (1927), 305–26. See Chapter 1,
in which I query the validity of the data.

CRANE, WILLIAM G. "Lord Berners' Translation of Diego de San
Pedro's *Cárcel de Amor*," *PMLA*, XLIX (1934), 1032–35. The
useful information is duplicated and amplified in his edition of
Lord Berners's translation: see below.

————. *Wit and Rhetoric in the Renaissance: The Formal Basis of
Elizabethan Prose Style* (New York: Columbia University Press,
1937). An extremely important and original work which deserves
to be much more widely known; gives considerable space to
both San Pedro's love stories.

————. *The Castle of Love, a Translation by John Bourchier* (Gaines-
ville, Florida: Scholars Facsimiles and Reprints, 1950). A facsimile of Lord Berners's translation of *Cárcel de Amor*, with
a long and useful introduction. Shows that Lord Berners worked
from a French translation, but had a Spanish edition to hand.

CUMMINS, J. S. See Whinnom, Keith.

DEYERMOND, A. D. "El hombre salvaje en la novela sentimental,"
Actas del Segundo Congreso Internacional de Hispanistas
(Nijmegen: Instituto Español de la Universidad de Nimega,
1967), 265–72. See below.

————. "El hombre salvaje en la novela sentimental," *Filología*, X
(1964), 97–111. An expanded version of the paper listed above;
traces the theme of hairy savages, and in discussing Desire in
Prison of Love sheds much light on San Pedro's conception
of love.

DURÁN, ARMANDO. *Estructura y técnicas de la novela sentimental y
caballeresca* (Madrid: Gredos, 1973). A Lévi-Strauss structuralist
approach, sometimes stimulating but often unsound; places
Arnalte and Lucenda and *Prison of Love* in different categories:
see Chapter 5.

EARLE, PETER G. "Love Concepts in *La Cárcel de Amor* and *La
Celestina*," *Hispania*, XXXIX (1956), 92–96. Picks out some
similarities and differences; interesting but slight.

FLIGHTNER, JAMES A. "The Popularity of the *Cárcel de Amor*,"
Hispania, XLVII (1964), 475–78. Negligible: not about its
popularity.

FOULCHÉ-DELBOSC, R. "Arnalte y Lucenda," *Revue Hispanique*, XXV

(1911), 220–82. In the introduction to this transcription of the edition of Burgos, 1522, Foulché-Delbosc gives the fullest bibliography up to that time of editions and translations of *Arnalte and Lucenda.*

GATTI, JOSÉ FRANCISCO. *Contribución al estudio de la "Cárcel de Amor": La apología de Leriano* (Buenos Aires: unsigned, 1955). Sources, antecedents, the feminist quarrel, etc.

GIANNINI, A. "La 'Cárcel de Amor' y el 'Cortegiano' de B. Castiglione," *Revue Hispanique*, XLVI (1919), 547–68. Argues that Castiglione was strongly influenced by San Pedro in writing *The Courtier.*

GILI Y GAYA, SAMUEL. Introduction to Diego de San Pedro, *Obras* (Madrid: Espasa-Calpe, 1950; 1958; 1967). A once useful but now outdated introduction to the author.

HARRIS, MARGARET A. *A Study of Théodose Valentinian's Amant resuscité de la mort d'amour: A Religious Novel of Sentiment and its Possible Connexions with Nicolas Denisot du Mans* (Geneva: Droz, 1966). Discusses in Chapter 3 the crucial influence of San Pedro, and especially *Arnalte and Lucenda*, on one of the earliest of the French "sentimental novels."

HOFFMEISTER, GERHART. "Diego de San Pedro und Hans Ludwig von Kufstein: Über eine frühbarocke Bearbeitung der spanischen Liebesgeschichte *Cárcel de amor*," *Arcadia*, VI (1971), 139–50. On the seventeenth-century German translation of *Prison of Love* and its influence on German literature.

KANY, CHARLES E. *The Beginnings of the Epistolary Novel in France, Italy and Spain* (Berkeley: University of California, 1937). Still the only study of its kind; he deals with both San Pedro's love stories in Chapter III: see Chapter 5 of this study.

KOSZUL, A. "La première traduction d'Arnalte et Lucenda et les débuts de la nouvelle sentimentale en Angleterre," *Études Littéraires: Mélanges, 1945* (Paris: Éditions Les Belles-Lettres, 1946), pp. 151–67. Self-explanatory but inexact title: he deals with the second English translation.

KRAUSE, ANNA. "La novela sentimental, 1440–1513." Unpublished dissertation, University of Chicago, 1927. A general survey, in general outdated.

––––. "Apunte bibliográfico sobre Diego de San Pedro," *Revista de Filología Española*, XXXVI (1952), 126–30. Describes an edition of *Prison of Love* with Nicolás Núñez's continuation in a California library.

––––. "El 'tractado' novelístico de Diego de San Pedro," *Bulletin Hispanique*, LIV (1952), 245–75. Argues that the key to understanding San Pedro's romances is the term *tractado* and the Latin didactic *tractatus*. See Chapter 5.

LANGBEHN-ROHLAND, REGULA. *Zur Interpretation der Romane des Diego de San Pedro* (Heidelberg: Carl Winter Universitätsverlag, 1970). By far the most thorough, substantial, and important study yet published of San Pedro's prose romances; indispensable for the serious student, despite certain errors and deficiencies, and some debatable propositions.

LIDA DE MALKIEL, MARÍA ROSA. *La originalidad artística de La Celestina* (Buenos Aires: Editorial Universitaria, 1962; 1970). Refers repeatedly to the heroes and heroines of San Pedro's romances in speaking of Calisto and Melibea.

MÁRQUEZ VILLANUEVA, F. "*Cárcel de amor,* novela política," *Revista de Occidente,* 2nd series, XIV (1966), 185–200. Argues for San Pedro's Jewish origins and interprets part of *Prison of Love* as a veiled protest against the Inquisition: see Chapter 1.

MENÉNDEZ PELAYO, MARCELINO. *Antología de poetas líricos castellanos.* 13 vols. (Madrid: Viuda de Hernando, 1890–1908; Edición Nacional, 10 vols., Santander: C.S.I.C., 1944–1945). In the latter edition, he deals with San Pedro, including his work in prose, in III, 167–83. Invaluable pioneering work, but no longer authoritative and far too frequently relied on.

————. *Orígenes de la novela.* 4 vols. Nueva Biblioteca de Autores Españoles, I, VII, XIV, and XXI (Madrid: Bailly-Baillière, 1905–1915; Edición Nacional, 4 vols., Santander: C.S.I.C., 1962). For San Pedro, see Vol. II of the Edición Nacional, 30–48. Repeats, sometimes word for word, the critical matter contained in *Antología* (see above), but introduces new (and incorrect) biographical information: see Chapter 1.

OOSTENDORP, H. T. *El conflicto entre el honor y el amor en la literatura española hasta el siglo XVII* (The Hague: Van Goor Zonen, 1962). Treats *Prison of Love* in terms of the motif of love versus honor.

PABST, WALTER. "Die Selbstbestrafung auf dem Stein," *Festgabe für Hellmuth Petriconi* (Hamburg: Cram, De Gruyter & Co., 1955), pp. 33–49. On allegory in *Prison of Love* as an antecedent for Don Quixote in the Sierra Morena. (Not seen.)

PÉREZ GÓMEZ, ANTONIO. " 'La pasión trobada' de Diego de San Pedro," *Revista de Literatura,* I (1952), 163–82. Photographic reproduction of the earliest extant *pliego* of *The Passion,* with an important pioneering bibliographical introduction; the preliminary essay is also of some historical importance, since Pérez Gómez was the first critic wholly to ignore the derogatory remarks habitually made about *The Passion* and proclaim its poetic merit.

REYNIER, GUSTAVE. *Le Roman sentimental avant l'Astrée* (Paris: Colin, 1908). Still not superseded in setting out in detail the importance of Spanish influences, and especially San Pedro, in the creation of the French "sentimental novel."

SAMONÀ, CARMELO. "Diego de San Pedro: dall'Arnalte e Lucenda alla Cárcel de amor," *Studi in onore di Pietro Silva* (Florence: Felice le Monnier, 1957), pp. 261–77. Examines the differences between the two novels and finds *Prison of Love* vastly superior.

————. *Studi sul romanzo sentimentale e cortese nella letteratura spagnola del Quattrocento* (Rome: Carucci, 1960). The first of two promised volumes; the second, which has not yet appeared, is to deal with Diego de San Pedro. This volume is useful for some of his precursors, and for its general observations about the genre.

SANPERE I MIQUEL, S. "Lo Carcer d'Amor de Diego de San Pedro: Edició catalana de Rosembach (Barcelona, 1493)," *Revista de Bibliografía Catalana*, II (1902), 46–84. A description of the early Catalan translation, which is now available in facsimile.

SCHEVILL, RUDOLPH. *Ovid and the Renascence in Spain* (Berkeley: University of California, 1913; repr. Hildesheim: Georg Olms, 1971). Fundamental for Ovidian reminiscences in Aenas Sylvius and San Pedro's *Arnalte and Lucenda*.

SERRANO PONCELA, S. "Dos 'Werther' del Renacimiento español," *Asomante*, V, 4 (1949), 87–103. Memorable only for perpetuating the unhelpful but inevitably-quoted reference to *Prison of Love* as the fifteenth-century *Werther*.

SEVERIN, DOROTHY S. See also Vivian, Dorothy S.

————. "The Earliest Version of Diego de San Pedro's 'La Pasión Trobada,'" *Romanische Forschungen*, LXXXI (1969), 176–92. A description, with a printing of the additional stanzas, of the version of *The Passion* in the "Cancionero de Oñate-Castañeda." Superseded by her palaeographic edition (see below).

————. *La Passión trobada de Diego de San Pedro: Edición paleográfica, según la versión manuscrita de Oñate-Castañeda* (Naples: Istituto Universitario Orientale di Napoli, 1974). Has, in addition to the text, a long and important introduction.

URQUIJO E IBARRA, JULIO DE. "Del teatro litúrgico en el País Vasco: 'La Passión Trobada' de Diego de San Pedro (representada en Lesaca en 1566)," *Revue Internationale des Études Basques*, XXII (1931), 150–218. Transcribes the text of *The Passion* and documents its dramatic performance in the Basque Provinces in the sixteenth century.

VARELA, JOSÉ LUIS. "Revisión de la novela sentimental," *Revista de Filología Española*, XLVIII (1965 [1967]), 351–82. A quite useful survey article which reiterates traditional views and does not really break new ground.

VIVIAN, DOROTHY SHERMAN. " 'La passión trobada' de Diego de San Pedro, y sus relaciones con el drama medieval de la Pasión," *Anuario de Estudios Medievales*, I (1964), 451–70. Traces numerous similarities between *The Passion* and medieval Passion plays. See Chapter 3.

WALEY, PAMELA. "Love and Honour in the *novelas sentimentales* of Diego de San Pedro and Juan de Flores," *Bulletin of Hispanic Studies*, XLIII (1966), 253–75. A useful comparison which reveals wide differences between two writers often grouped together; the author shows a distinct preference for Juan de Flores.

WARDROPPER, BRUCE W. "Allegory and the Role of 'el Autor' in the 'Cárcel de Amor,' " *Philological Quarterly*, XXXI (1952), 39–44. See below.

———. "El mundo sentimental de la *Cárcel de Amor*," *Revista de Filología Española*, XXXVII (1953), 168–93. Two articles originally conceived and written as one and split by editorial exigency. A huge step forward in the appreciation of *Prison of Love*; one may quarrel with sundry particulars, but these articles lifted criticism of San Pedro onto a new plane.

WHINNOM, KEITH. "Was Diego de San Pedro a *converso*? A Re-examination of Cotarelo's Documentary Evidence," *Bulletin of Hispanic Studies*, XXXIV (1957), 187–200. Queries the validity of the evidence and conclusions of Cotarelo. See Chapter 1.

WHINNOM, KEITH and CUMMINS, S. J. "An Approximate Date for the Death of Diego de San Pedro," *Bulletin of Hispanic Studies*, XXXVI (1959), 226–29. The evidence and arguments are invalidated by the confusion of two different San Pedros. See Chapter 1.

WHINNOM, KEITH. "The Religious Poems of Diego de San Pedro: Their Relationship and Their Dating," *Hispanic Review*, XXVIII (1960), 1–15. Examines the chronology and dating of *The Passion* and *The Seven Sorrows*.

———. "Diego de San Pedro's Stylistic Reform," *Bulletin of Hispanic Studies*, XXXVII (1960), 1–15. Examines in medieval rhetorical terms the differences between the style of *Arnalte and Lucenda* and *Prison of Love*. See Chapter 5.

—————. "The First Printing of San Pedro's *Passión trobada*," *Hispanic Review*, XXX (1962), 149–51. On the Hurus *cancioneros* of 1492 and 1495.

—————. "The Supposed Sources of Inspiration of Spanish Fifteenth-century Narrative Religious Verse," *Symposium*, Winter 1963, 268–91. Looks at the alleged influence of the *devotio moderna* and Ludolph of Saxony, and draws attention to the importance of the *Meditationes vitae Christi*. See Chapter 3.

—————. "Two San Pedros," *Bulletin of Hispanic Studies*, XLII (1965), 255–88. Rejects the identification of the author with the *bachiller*. See Chapter 1.

—————. "Lucrezia Borgia and a Lost Edition of Diego de San Pedro's *Arnalte y Lucenda*," *Annali del Istituto Universitario Orientale di Napoli: Sezione Romanza*, XIII (1971), 143–51. Shows that a MS. poem in praise of Lucrezia Borgia is a plagiarism of San Pedro's poem in praise of Isabella, and that readings and arrangement of stanzas which agree with the Burgos, 1522, edition, as against the 1491 edition of *Arnalte y Lucenda*, indicate a lost intermediate edition.

—————. "The Mysterious Marina Manuel (Prologue, *Cárcel de Amor*)," *Studia Iberica: Festschrift für Hans Flasche* (Berne and Munich: Francke, 1973), pp. 689–95. See Chapter 1.

—————. "Nicolás Núñez's Continuation of the *Cárcel de Amor*," *Studies in Spanish Literature of the Golden Age Presented to Edward M. Wilson* (London: Tamesis Books, 1973), 357–66. Suggests that *Prison of Love* may not have been properly understood or appreciated by San Pedro's contemporaries.

Index

Note that names and topics which occur in the Notes are not indexed when the reader will be led to them by the primary reference in the text.

166

DIEGO DE SAN PEDRO

asticus, Genesis, Isaiah, Jeremiah, Job, John, Luke, Maccabees, Mark, Matthew, Peter
Boabdil, K. of Granada, 25
Bobadilla, Beatriz de, 135n20
Boccaccio, 7; *Decameron*, 79, 114; *De casibus*, 127; *Fiammetta*, 78, 79
Boethius, 126-29 passim, 131
Bonaventure, St., 42. *See also Meditationes vitae Christi*
Boscán, Juan, 28, 33, 52, 131
Bourchier, John. *See* Berners, Lord
Brethren of the Common Life, 47
buen gusto, 114
Burgos, *bachiller*, 45
Burgundy, Baldwin of, 26; Charles the Bold of, 26

caballeros salvajes, 149n1
Calatrava, Order of, 23, 24
Calixtus III, Pope, 23
Callimachus, 75
Cancionero de Baena, 55
Cancionero de Hurus, 59
Cancionero de Oñate-Castañeda, 36, 37, 56-57
Cancionero general, 8, 125
cancionero poetry, 122-24
captatio benevolentiae, 69
Cárcel de Amor. See Prison of Love
Caro Baroja, Julio, 135n17
Carrillo, Alfonso, Archbishop of Toledo, 24
Cartagena, poet, 27
Castiglione, Baldesar, 152n41
Castile, in fifteenth century, 29-32
Catalonia, in fifteenth century, 30
Celestina, 8, 9, 33, 82, 117, 131
Ceyx, 147n26
Charland, Th.-M., 149n3
Charles the Bold of Burgundy, 26
Chaucer, 114
Chrétien de Troyes, 73
Christ. *See* Bible, *Compassio Mariae*, Crucifixion, Flagellation, *imitatio Christi*, Passion
Cicero, 71, 114

Cid. *See Mocedades de Rodrigo*
Cohn, Norman, 142n23
colloquia personarum. See dialogue
colores rhetorici, anglice colours of rhetoric, 85-86
comic elements, in *Arnalte and Lucenda*, 72-75, 80; in the *Sermon*, 94-95
Common Life, Brethren of the, 47
comparatio, 115, 120
Compassio Mariae, 40, 42, 56, 140-n13
Condestable. *See* Constable
Constable of Castile, Pedro Fernández de Velasco, 24, 136n32
Constable of Portugal, Dom Pedro, author of *Sátira de felice e infelice vida*, 76, 78
Contempt of Fortune, analysis of, 126-29; referred to, 18, 22, 27, 28, 35, 36, 72
contrasti, 70
conversos, 19-22 passim, 29. *See also* Jews
Corinthians, First Epistle to the, 141n5
Cotarelo y Mori, Emilio, 20-22 passim, 136n29
courtly love, 88-91, 92-93, 103, 149n5
Crane, W. G., 146n14
Crucifixion, 41-42, 49, 53, 56, 57. *See also* Passion
Cuestión de amor, 76
Cueva, Beltrán de la, 23
Cummins, J. S., 137n39
Cvitanovic, D., 77

Dante, 52, 109, 114, 126, 151n17
Darbord, Michel, 45, 52
Decameron. See Boccaccio
De casibus virorum et feminarum illustrium. See Boccaccio
Desprecio de la Fortuna. See Contempt of Fortune
devotio moderna, 139n6, 140n13
Deyermond, A. D., 147n35, 149n1, 152n29

Index   **169**